IMAGES
of Aviation

CENTRAL OREGON
AVIATION

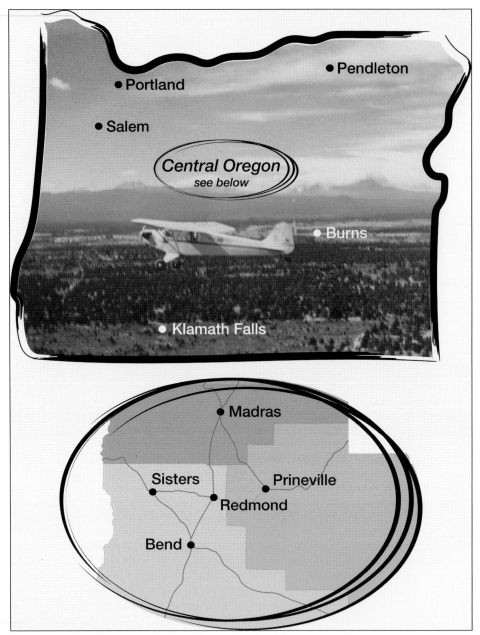

The majestic Cascade Mountains provide a fitting backdrop to Bend Flying Service's Piper J3C-65S soaring over Central Oregon in the early 1940s. The mountains were a formidable obstacle between the rural communities of Redmond, Bend, and Sisters in Deschutes County; Madras in Jefferson County; Prineville in Crook County; and the large commercial and political centers west of the Cascades. Local officials and business leaders understood early on the role of the airplane in shortening the daylong travel times of railroads and automobiles. (Prineville Crook County Airport.)

ON THE COVER: Sporting the latest fashions, Portland-based pilot Lee Meadows (far right), the copilot (second from right) and their passengers pose in front of a Fairchild Model 17 at Bend's Long Butte airport in the mid-1930s. (Deschutes Historical Museum.)

IMAGES
of Aviation

CENTRAL OREGON
AVIATION

Tor Hanson

ARCADIA
PUBLISHING

Published by Arcadia Publishing
Charleston, South Carolina

Printed in the United States of America

Library of Congress Control Number: 2021947657

For all general information, please contact Arcadia Publishing:
Telephone 843-853-2070
Fax 843-853-0044
E-mail sales@arcadiapublishing.com
For customer service and orders:
Toll-Free 1-888-313-2665

Visit us on the Internet at www.arcadiapublishing.com

This book is dedicated to my mom, Gun, an accomplished writer in her own right, who taught me how to put together an eye-catching lede.

CONTENTS

ACKNOWLEDGMENTS

Bulltofta, the mostly forgotten city airport of Malmö, Sweden, was still in service in the 1960s when I grew up. Close to the runway was a hill where people could watch airplanes take off and land. One day my dad, Kjell, took my brother Jörgen and me to experience the thrill of airplane spotting. I may have been 10 or 11 years old.

In the distance, a Scandinavian Airlines Convair Metropolitan, a two-propeller aircraft, lined up on the runway, nose pointed directly at the observation spot.

With brakes on, the pilot gunned the engines for takeoff. The sound of the propellers changed from a buzzing whine to a full-on roar. The entire airplane shook. The pilot released the brakes. The seemingly small airplane became larger, approaching us with alarming speed.

I do not remember how high the "hill" was, but staring at the oncoming airplane, I wondered if it was going to clear the obstacle and us standing there watching. The Metropolitan's silvery aluminum belly slid effortlessly across the hill, wheels retracting into the wings and fuselage. The roar was deafening. At that moment, I threw myself on the ground, hands over my ears, and started crying. I have been a passionate aviation enthusiast ever since.

Hats off to Les Joslin and Lance Judd, good friends and fellow writers, who proofread the book; Prineville Crook County Airport manager Kelly Coffelt and Steve Lent from the Bowman Museum in Prineville; Margaret Schinkel, granddaughter of J.R. Roberts, who gave me access to her grandfather's correspondence and photo albums; Kay Kirkbride, who supplied material about her father, Ollie Bowman; June Butler Jaeger, who gave me access to photographs and documents about her father, Calvin Butler; Jarold Ramsey, who helped me with photographs and history about Madras Airport; and City of Prineville senior planner Casey Kaiser, who launched a drone to take new aerial photographs of the airport.

Over the years, I have interviewed Central Oregon residents about their aviation experiences. Thanks to Neil Farnham, Leon Devereaux, Phil Peoples, and Jim Hosmer. The information about Rex Barber comes from a 1992 interview conducted at his home in Terrebonne.

Also, thanks to Kelly Cannon-Miller, Rebekah Averette, and Vanessa Ivey at the Deschutes Historical Museum for giving me access to the museum's photographic holdings. These photographs are credited DHM.

INTRODUCTION

Central Oregon was settled in the late 1800s. Pioneers were attracted to the area and the promise of 160 acres of land, as set out in the Homestead Act of 1864. In the early days, the only ways to access the high desert were oxen- or horse-drawn wagons. As the area gained a stable population, sheep- and cattle-ranchers, as well as farmers in Wasco County, needed reliable means to get wool, livestock, and wheat to the markets on the other side of the Cascades.

In May 1900, the railroad reached Shaniko, Oregon. However, travel to the small towns in Oregon's interior was still a time-consuming endeavor. A trip via stagecoach from Shaniko to Redmond or Bend was measured in days on dusty roads.

Far away, on the Outer Banks in North Carolina, two brothers were fine-tuning an invention that would transform transportation. But in 1903, not even the Wright brothers knew what to make of their "aeroplane." With large Midwestern lumber companies buying up thousands of acres of forest land in Central Oregon in the early 1900s, the urgency to establish a railroad became of utmost importance. Progress had to wait until 1911 when a subsidiary of Union Pacific Railroad finally pushed into the area. Travel became far more comfortable, but speed was still an issue. Portland and Salem were almost a full day away, even by train.

Not much changed in the development of the airplane up until World War I. From 1914 through 1918, the Wright brothers' invention went from a curiosity to a capable war machine. The Germans and the French had already overtaken the United States in the development of the airplane.

A late entrant in the war, the United States had to do battle with French SPADs and Nieuports, or British DeHavilland airplanes. The only aircraft development coming out of the United States was the military trainer Curtiss JN-4, nicknamed the "Jenny."

When the hostilities ended on November 11, 1918, thousands of American pilots returned home. Working on establishing the League of Nations and a world of peace and prosperity, Pres. Woodrow Wilson drastically pulled back on military development.

At the same time, surplus Jennies went up for sale. Former military pilots scooped up the airplanes on the cheap. To make a buck or two, they visited every corner of the country where there was an open field that could be used as a landing strip. People flocked to these barnstorming pilots to take a quick flight above their hometown.

The Central Oregon landscape can most easily be described as a high desert. The landing fields carved out of the desert were covered with fine dust and sharp volcanic rocks—a rough place to bring down a Jenny. On the other hand, the area was ideal for flying. The weather patterns provided plenty of sunny days.

The 1920 US Census put Bend as the largest city in the Central Oregon area with a population of 5,415. Prineville had 1,144; Redmond, 585; and Madras, 337. Looking at the census from a different perspective, Deschutes, Crook, and Jefferson Counties had a total population of 16,257. As a comparison, more than 258,000 people lived in Portland at the time.

Early on, the Bend Commercial Club understood the advantages of aviation. The fledgling technology promised a quick hop over the mountains to commercial centers like Portland and Eugene, and Oregon's political center—Salem.

In February 1918, Col. George Crabtree of the US Army Air Corps at Spokane, Washington, was on an inspection trip to Portland to look for suitable space for a flying school. Colonel Crabtree was not impressed with Portland weather, according to an article in *The Bend Bulletin* on February 5, 1918: "It is evident that Portland and contiguous territory cannot compete for flying schools owing to fog and rain and a minimum of clear days."

H.J. Overturf of the Bend Commercial Club immediately sent a telegram to Colonel Crabtree, reading, "Respectfully call attention to superior advantages of Sunny Bend for location of such institutions. Our facilities are yours. Please command us."

In a letter to US senator Charles McNary of Oregon, the Bend Commercial Club pointed out that Central Oregon had "the largest area of cleared level land in the state." The letter continued, "We respectfully request that the merits of this location be put before the proper authorities."

On April 18, 1918, Senator McNary replied, "Some days ago Senator [George] Chamberlain, Representative [Nicholas] Sinnott, and myself, requested the aviation department to locate one or more aviation camps in Oregon. I shall present your claim and personally speak most favorably of the district as a site for an aviation camp."

With McNary's gambit, Central Oregon got on the radar of the western locating board headquartered in San Diego, California. In April 1918, it was announced that representatives were scheduled to visit Oregon. Unfortunately, neither Bend, Redmond, or Prineville were selected.

In August 1919, *The Bend Bulletin* published an editorial headlined "A Landing Field." The writer asked if the matter of obtaining an airfield was the responsibility of the Bend Commercial Club, the city council, or the general public. They considered it doubtful the club was the right organization to procure an airfield.

Perhaps upset with this editorial, the Bend Commercial Club created an aviation field committee. In February 1920, the club paid for a government aviation expert to help identify locations for a landing field. The aviation field committee favored a site southeast of town. A month later, the landing field became known as Knotts Field.

Redmond had a similar low-key approach to aviation. Aircraft enthusiasts and, to a certain degree, city officials saw a need for investing in airfield infrastructure.

Redmond's first airfield was attached to the fairgrounds. Located on the west side of the Dalles-California Highway—where one can find the Fred Meyer store today—city officials blessed the idea of a landing field, and 40 acres were put aside.

It was into this interior area of Oregon the likes of Silas Christofferson, the Thompson brothers, Lawrence Sohler, and many others came to ply their craft as aviators and spread the "winged gospel." More than 100 years later, they would be surprised at what came of their efforts.

One

IT'S IN THE AIR

It would be impossible to write about aviation without mentioning Wilbur and Orville Wright. Their 120-foot flight on December 17, 1903, at Kitty Hawk, North Carolina, started an unprecedented development of a brand-new technology that continues to this day.

News of the Wright brothers and the development of the airplane made the newspapers in faraway rural Oregon. *The Bend Bulletin* reported aviation firsts on a regular basis: The world's first known airplane fatality was dutifully reported—US Army lieutenant Thomas Selfridge, who died in a crash at Fort Myer on September 17, 1908, was a passenger in a Wright Flyer piloted by Orville Wright. Orville's "perfect aeroplane flight" at Fort Myer on July 2, 1909, was also written up, as well as Bleirot's cross-channel flight between France and England on July 27, 1909, and Glenn Curtiss's record-breaking flight from Albany to New York City on May 31, 1910. Wilbur Wright's death on May 30, 1912, passed by unnoticed.

Only nine years after the Wright brothers' successful first flight in 1903, the first recorded flights in Central Oregon took place at the Crook County Fairgrounds in Prineville. It made sense. At the time, Prineville was the seat of Crook County, which also included what in 1916 became Deschutes County.

If there were other airplanes visiting Central Oregon at the time, the historical records are lacking. Perhaps World War I came in between, and the 1918 influenza pandemic certainly did not help.

On the rear side of World War I, the airplane was no longer a "seat-of-your-pants" invention. Aircraft companies were building increasingly more sophisticated crafts. The US Army trainer, the Curtiss JN-4 Jenny, became a barnstormer's dream.

In 12 seconds that changed the world, on December 17, 1903, Orville and Wilbur Wright became the first to fly a powered, heavier-than-air airplane. Orville is piloting the Wright Flyer in this photograph, and Wilbur is running at the wingtip. The image was recorded by John T. Daniels of the US Life-Saving Service crew at Kill Devil Hills. (Library of Congress.)

The US Army Signal Corps became the Wright brothers' first customer. As part of the sales agreement, Orville Wright instructed two military officers to pilot the airplane, lieutenants Frederic Humphreys and Frank Lahm. In 1909, the US Army established College Park Aviation Field in Maryland as a training ground for the pilots. This photograph shows a B-version of the Wright Flyer piloted by Lt. Harry T. Graham. (Library of Congress.)

In time for the annual Crook County Fair in 1912, Silas Christofferson became the first aviator to bring an airplane to Central Oregon. According to the Thursday, October 17, 1912, edition of the *Crook County Journal*, aviator Christofferson could not wait to get his Curtiss biplane airborne: "About five o'clock Tuesday evening a whirr and a whizz informed the dickybirds and magpies that their monopoly of Crook County's atmosphere had been 'busted.' The big mechanical bird and the men who have tamed it are big drawing cards [at the fair]." Below is an aerial view of Crook County Fairgrounds at a later date. The landing field used for Christofferson's airplane was by then filled with houses. (Above, Bowman Museum; below, Prineville Crook County Airport.)

Prineville, Ore. Oct. 16-19, 12

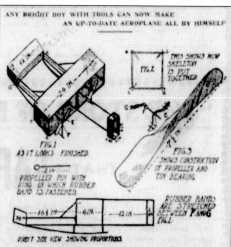

The first airplane-induced accident in Central Oregon also took place at the 1912 fair. Showing off his skills to the audience, Christofferson swooped low to the ground. Unfortunately, a wingtip struck Stowell Cram in the face. He lingered for two days at a hospital before passing away on October 18, 1912. The aviator was "all broken up about the accident," according to the local newspaper. (Bowman Museum.)

The newspapers fanned the Central Oregon "air craze." This ad in the April 10, 1910, issue of *The Bend Bulletin*, promised "any bright boy with tools can now make an up-to-date aeroplane all by himself." All that was needed to build a flyer was a bamboo fishing pole cut to length, linen strings, and light linen cloth painted with a mixture of paraffin dissolved in benzine. (DHM.)

Two

BARNSTORMERS
AND AIR CIRCUS

If stunt flying in early airplanes was not enough to draw big crowds, barnstormers often added attractions to keep the excitement going. Wing walking was a sure-fire crowd-pleaser, as was parachute jumping, or hanging upside down from wings or wheel braces.

Central Oregon got caught up in the air craze after initial visits from barnstormers like the Thompson brothers and Lt. Archie F. Roth.

Visiting aviators were front-page news. One of the more prolific barnstormers was Tex Rankin. His air circus had top billing in the fall of 1924. Advertised as "the Quinn-Rankin flyers," the group pulled out all the stunts. They also offered sightseeing flights over Bend. The newspaper promised "Flying, Weather Permitting." Children under 10 paid $2.50, while adults paid $5 to see "the mountains and the beautiful country from the air."

Even the Catholic church in Bend asked for help from up above. When the Catholic bazaar in Bend needed advertising, they chartered an airplane to drop tickets over Bend. The numbered cards corresponded with prizes displayed at Cashman's store, among them 10 toy airplanes.

Rankin returned to Bend as Bookwalter & Rankin—"the Northwest's Pioneer Airmen." Their October 1925 ad in the local newspaper promised "Stunts All Day." The pioneer airmen performed wing walking, a sensational 3,000-foot parachute leap, and a landing with the motor dead.

Parachutist Harold Groves caused more than enough excitement for the 4,000 spectators gathered to see the air circus. After Groves jumped from the airplane, his parachute closed, causing the jumper to experience a 1,500-foot freefall before the parachute opened again.

The antics of the barnstormer years sound unbelievable today. One way to experience the thrills offered by Rankin and his vagabond flyers is to watch perhaps one of the best movies chronicling the time, the 1975 drama *The Great Waldo Pepper*.

One of the first barnstormer visits after the war took place at the Interstate Fair in Prineville on October 1–4, 1919. The Ace Aircraft Corporation of Portland plastered the local newspapers in Prineville and Bend with ads promising "daily thrilling stunt flights" in the *Ace-O'-Hearts*, piloted by Lt. Archie F. Roth. According to a September 25, 1919, *Crook County Journal* article, the pilot saw "more than 400 hours service above the battle lines in France." There was no lack of customers willing to pay $1 a minute to see Prineville from above. "Flying is a wonderful sensation," said local attorney Marion Elliott to the Prineville newspaper. "I have long promised myself this experience the first opportunity that offered, and as this was the first chance, I accepted it." (Both, DHM.)

Signed by Pres. William Taft, Edward Knotts was granted a patent on 200 acres on February 7, 1913. It is not known why Knotts decided to open his property to a small airfield. With the potential to become Bend's first landing field, the Bend Commercial Club put together an aviation field committee in February 1920 under the leadership of Norman Jacobson, US Forest Service supervisor of the Deschutes National Forest. The club paid a government aviation expert to identify desirable locations for a landing field. In late March 1920, N.B. Evans surveyed several sites and settled on Knotts's property. *The Bend Bulletin* reported, "It is some 160 acres in extent, and rough estimates place its probable cost at $5,000. To put the ground in proper shape for the landing and starting of airplanes would cost in the neighborhood of $1,000." These photographs were taken at Knotts Field in 1920. (Both, DHM.)

The Jenny became the preferred airplane for barnstormers. The Curtiss Aeroplane Company in Hammondsport, New York, built the training aircraft for the US Army. With the end of World War I, there was a huge surplus of aircraft and engines. When the government began selling off the excess inventory, a Curtiss JN-4H trainer with an engine could be had for a mere $300. (Tonia Kissler Cain.)

Bend and Redmond's first close-up experience with an airplane took place in early May 1920 when Roland Thompson's Curtiss JN-4 touched down in Redmond as part of a Central Oregon barnstorming tour. And on Saturday, May 8, Bend folks got to see Thompson's Jenny flying over Knotts Field, a cleared part of Edward Knotts' dairy farm. (DHM.)

Over the weekend, 27 daring residents took the chance to see the city from above. *The Bend Bulletin* reported that one of Thompson's passengers steadied his nerves with Prohibition-era "hootch" during the flight: "Under the influence of the stimulant, the aerial joy rider decided that it would be well for him to walk about a bit and unbuckled his life belt before Thompson could interfere. He was promptly jerked to his seat." (DHM.)

Neil Farnham was 12 years old when he and his brother Willard were seated in a barnstormer's airplane in the early 1930s. "The pilot charged by the pound," said Farnham in a 2010 interview. "It was a penny a pound. The flight cost me 96¢. The pilot put my brother and I in the front seat. We took off, flew around the field, and landed again." (DHM.)

Frank Prince (left) was the editor of the lumber firm Shevlin-Hixon's newsletter, *Shevlin Equalizer*, and Paul Hosmer (center) was the editor of Brooks-Scanlon's newsletter, *Pine Echoes*. They were inseparable and not ones to miss an opportunity for adventure. Although there is no date for this photograph, based on articles in *The Bend Bulletin*, it was likely taken in June 1920. The pilot is possibly Larry Sohler. (DHM.)

Barnstormer Tex Rankin and his brother Dick staged a flying circus in Bend on October 24, 1924. An ad in *The Bend Bulletin* promised great fun: "Dick Rankin will hang by his toes from the landing gear and perform many hair-raising stunts from the wings of the airplane." Here, Rankin is seen with his cat Jinx, proving, without a doubt, that flying is safe—even with a black cat in the cockpit. (DHM.)

Three

AN UNEXPECTED ALLIANCE

With the barnstormer years in full swing, horrified airplane manufacturers and airline executives began questioning the federal government's laissez-faire attitude to air commerce. The barnstormers and their "devil-may-care" attitude did little to make the general public see the airplane as anything but a circus act.

There was a need to instill confidence among the public that the airplane was a safe transportation mode. Much of the bad reputation was attributed to less safety-conscious barnstormers who racked up an ever-mounting number of airplane accidents, many with a deadly outcome.

In a 1921 letter to New York congressman Fredrick Hicks, secretary of commerce Herbert Hoover mused, "It is interesting to note that this is the only industry that favors itself regulated by government."

In 1924, a mere two decades after the Wright brothers' first flight, the airplane was still thought of as having limited commercial application. "For the most part, people thought of flying as somewhere between a sport and a side show," said William P. McCracken Jr., who soon became the first US assistant secretary of commerce for aeronautics.

On the urgings of the aviation industry, the federal government laid the foundation for a regulated commercial air transportation industry.

Several bills were developed in the Senate. One major concern was that the states would not allow federal regulation to take precedence over the states' right to control aviation. After a protracted battle in Congress, the final sticking points were ironed out in 1926. Pres. Calvin Coolidge signed the Air Commerce Act on May 20, 1926. It established the Aeronautics Branch as an entity within the US Department of Commerce.

The focus of the newly created branch was air safety, establishing airways, providing adequate air navigation aids along the routes, and investigating accidents. With the act in place, the barnstorming years effectively came to an end in 1926.

With the signing of the Air Commerce Act of 1926, the federal government again punted on who was going to pay for the development of safe airports. Without money to develop a robust airport infrastructure, cities like Bend, Redmond, Madras, and Prineville continued to use unimproved fields around Central Oregon. This photograph was taken east of Bend with Pilot Butte, a familiar landmark, barely visible to the left. (DHM.)

Early airplanes had a less than stellar safety record, and an inexperienced pilot in the cockpit made things worse. The Central Oregon high desert had another drawback. At 3,600 feet above sea level, the air was thinner. An airplane rated for two passengers plus the pilot at Portland could only carry one passenger in Bend. Long takeoffs with an underpowered and overloaded airplane could quickly spell trouble. (DHM.)

In the early 1920s, airplane accidents made national news on an ongoing basis. Barnstorming and other commercial enterprises were taking a toll, in both lives and customer confidence. Between 1921 and 1925, a total of 354 people perished nationally. Apart from the incident at the Crook County Fair in 1912, no deadly accidents took place in Central Oregon up to 1925. (DHM.)

World War I aviator and Chicago attorney William P. McCracken Jr. (standing) was appointed by US secretary of commerce Herbert Hoover in 1926 to lead the newly created Aeronautics Branch. McCracken became a dominant force in creating federal regulations for the rapidly developing "air commerce," which addressed establishing airways, licensing pilots, and issuing airworthiness certificates for aircraft. (Putnam Museum and Science Center, Davenport, Iowa.)

A momentous event affected the world of aviation in the latter part of the Roaring Twenties—the solo crossing of the Atlantic by former airmail pilot Charles Lindbergh in his airplane the *Spirit of St. Louis*. Lindbergh flew his specially equipped Ryan monoplane across the Atlantic in 33.5 hours, landing at Le Bourget Aerodrome in Paris on May 21, 1927. Unlike the Wright brothers' first flight, which took several years to hit the newspapers, Lindbergh's transatlantic flight was an overnight sensation and became front-page news in both *The Bend Bulletin* and *The Redmond Spokesman*. With Lindbergh's flight fresh in memory and the potential for commercial aviation to bring tourism dollars into the area, city councils in Bend and Redmond began the process of finding alternatives to the landing fields at Knotts Ranch and the Redmond Fairground. (Left, Library of Congress; below, *The Bend Bulletin*.)

In the aftermath of Lindbergh's flight across the Atlantic in the *Spirit of St. Louis,* pictured above at the Smithsonian National Air & Space Museum in Washington, DC, Central Oregon citizens got a chance to see a similar airplane up-close on Wednesday, September 7, 1927. The *Queen of the Yukon* was advertised as a "sister ship to Col. Lindbergh's Spirit of St. Louis." On a delivery flight to Whitehorse, Alaska, for Yukon Airways and Exploration Company, the plane was piloted by A.D. Cruikshank and William A. Monday with Clyde G. Wann, vice president of the company, as a passenger. Perhaps to bring in extra cash to defray the cost of gasoline, the plane landed at Knotts Field and the owners immediately offered exhibition flights to interested Oregonians. (Above, Ad Meskens under CC BY-SA 3.0; below, Alamy Stock Photo.)

As flying gained a more solid reputation, cities began expanding their airport offerings. With Knotts Field a temporary solution, Bend officials began looking for a larger site to develop an airport. In June 1931, city officials purchased E.H. Brandenburg's property north of Bend, creating the Long Butte Airport, seen above. The location was not ideal. Long Butte, a volcanic cinder butte, rose to the northeast of the landing field. The road leading to the airport on the west side had a long line of overhead wires, visible below. At a city council meeting on June 7, 1939, the Bend Flying Club asked the city to lower the telephone line, saying, "It rendered the east-west runway useless." (Above, Bend–Fort Rock Ranger District, Deschutes National Forest; below, Donna Rustland.)

Knotts Field and Long Butte Airport co-existed for many years. This photograph shows Robert D. Bedinger, inspector with the Department of Commerce Aeronautics Branch–Western Region, at Knotts Field. The Waco Aircraft Company of Troy, Ohio, manufactured a wide range of civilian biplanes. Bedinger's Waco UEC came with a 210 horsepower Continental R-670 engine and could carry a pilot and three passengers. (DHM.)

Although no pictures show the original Redmond landing field, this is where the dreams of an airport started—the Deschutes County Fairgrounds. A work crew cleared a landing area, cutting down four trees and leveling the ground. In mid-August 1920, *The Redmond Spokesman* reported, "An eight-foot white muslin flag to indicate the direction of the wind, has been hung from one of the flagpoles on the fair ground grandstand." (DHM.)

In the late 1920s and early 1930s, larger passenger airplanes were developed in both Europe and the United States. In Germany, Junkers produced the W33, an all-metal aircraft, which in 1930 led to the development of the Junkers Ju 52/3m. Ford entered the airplane manufacturing business in 1926 with an all-metal passenger aircraft, the Ford Trimotor (pictured), which could send 12 passengers aloft in relative safety—for the era. (DHM.)

Bend held a rip-roaring Airplane Dance on April 30, 1930, to celebrate the arrival of a Trimotor at Knotts Field. Named the *West Wind*, this Trimotor was owned by the Mamer Flying Service of Spokane, Washington. It was stationed in Hawaii during the attack on Pearl Harbor. Re-christened the *City of Richmond*, it sold for $1.2 million in 1969 and is still in flying condition. (DHM.)

Prineville residents also got bitten by the aviation bug in the early 1920s. A *Crook County Journal* article in May 1920 mentioned a landing field at the old Cross Place "at the head of the new grade west of town." The lower landing field is seen above. The 40-acre property again made the news in April 1931, when the City of Prineville purchased the tract after a lobbying campaign by the Prineville Businessmen's Club. An article in the April 16, 1931, *Central Oregonian* reported, "Visiting airmen praised the location of the Prineville aeronautical field." It would take another three years before the first official airfield was constructed with help from the Civil Works Administration (CWA). (Both, Bowman Museum.)

In February 1934, the *Central Oregonian* reported that 91 men were working on clearing the sagebrush on the property to construct a 4,400-foot graveled runway. The airport was dedicated on August 30, 1934, when local resident Lt. Wistar Rosenberg (center above) landed his US Army airplane at the new field. Pilot Rosenberg and his passenger, Capt. Harry Killpack, would later perish in a horrific crash in their O-19B Army observation biplane at the airport on August 29, 1935 (below). After taking off from the field, heading toward Pearson Field in Washington, Rosenberg was unable to gain altitude and crashed west of the airport. Rosenberg's father, Dr. John Rosenberg, witnessed the crash and was one of the first to reach the wreck. (Above, Bowman Museum; below, DHM.)

Four

IN THEIR FLYING MACHINES

The aircraft presented in this chapter capture the beauty of the well-known as well as the odd machines that buzzed the Central Oregon skies during the 1930s.

American airplane manufacturers such as Piper, Taylorcraft Aviation, Alexander Eaglerock, Cessna, Fairchild, Aeronca, and Waco turned out a dizzying multitude of aircraft in the pre–World War II years. Many of the companies, which produced military aircraft during the war, returned to the civilian market after hostilities ended.

A great number of the aircraft in the following photographs would go on to become "classic aircraft," with a fan base far beyond the 1930s and 1940s. Several of the airplanes pictured here are still in flying condition. Others were one-offs, developed by inventors and engineers who plied their craft but whose designs, for whatever reason, did not catch on.

As the blockbuster 1961 movie *Those Magnificent Men in Their Flying Machines* alludes to, the lion's share of aviators in the early 1920s and 1930s were men. Period photographs from Central Oregon show men and their aircraft at local airports. This is not to say female aviators were not making their marks. In the early days of aviation, women had few role models, but as aviatrixes like Amelia Earhart, Bessie Coleman, Pancho Barnes, and Anne Morrow Lindbergh began making their presence known, women saw a future in aviation. Earhart was one of the founding members of Ninety-Nines: International Organization of Women Pilots, an organization that supported the advancement of women pilots.

Several local women pilots made their marks in the annals of Central Oregon aviation. The co-publisher of *The Redmond Spokesman*, Mary Brown was heavily involved in local aviation as an aviatrix as well as an opinion builder. And Helen Skjersaa left Bend for the University of Idaho to earn her pilot license. She later became part of the Women Airforce Service Pilots corps.

The Brunner-Winkle Aircraft Company of Glendale, New York, produced a total of 200 aircraft from 1928 to 1931, marketed under the name Bird. The Bird was crowned the winner of the 1929 Guggenheim Safety Award as the safest production aircraft. Anne Morrow Lindbergh was taught to fly in a Bird by her husband, Charles. This CK model, with tail No. N818W, was manufactured in 1930 and is still in flying condition. (DHM.)

Another visitor to Bend's airport was this Piper Aircraft J-3C-65, manufactured in 1939, with tail number NC22973. The Cub is one of the company's most endearing favorites. The twin-seater has been described as simple and lightweight. Piper built nearly 20,000 Cubs between 1938 and 1947. During its tenure in Central Oregon, this airplane was stationed in Prineville as a trainer. It is still flying. (DHM.)

This seven-seat Fairchild Model 17, tail number NC9734, is one of the larger airplanes showing up at Bend's Long Butte Airport. Manufactured in December 1928 by the Fairchild Airplane Manufacturing Corporation, Lionel T. Barneson of Los Angeles, California, purchased the plane for $18,400. His father, Capt. John Barneson, was the founder of General Petroleum and built California's first pipeline. The airplane arrived in California aboard the steamship SS *Dakotan*. During the Great Depression, the Fairchild was bought and sold 13 times. At some point between 1931 and 1938, it was owned by James Lester "Lee" Meadows of Portland (far right below). Meadows was inducted into the Oregon Aviation Hall of Fame in 2014. Although no records exist of who his passengers were, this image captures the fashions of the 1930s—pilots and passengers alike. (Both, DHM.)

This Airster S-1 was designed by Bert Kinner and produced by his Security National Aircraft Corporation. The prototype took flight in 1933, in the throes of the Great Depression. Only 12 production models were built, and the company stopped production in 1935. One of the Airsters was sold to Edgar Rice Burroughs, author of the *Tarzan* books. Pictured is pilot Art Whitaker's airplane at Bend's Long Butte Airport. (DHM.)

Great Lakes Aircraft Company of Cleveland, Ohio, produced 32 Great Lakes TG-2s in the early 1930s. The company would go on to build torpedo bombers and dive bombers for the US Navy. This airplane, with tail number NC807Y, belonged to Clarence Bell. The photograph shows Bell and an unidentified mechanic gassing up the plane using jerry cans. (DHM.)

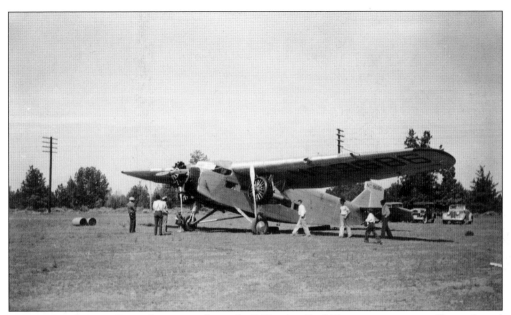

Visiting Bend's Long Butte Airport in the early 1930s, this Ford Trimotor was originally purchased by Los Angeles–based Maddux Air Lines. In November 1929, Transcontinental Air Transport (TAT) bought the company, and a year later, TAT-Maddux merged with Western Air Express, forming the nucleus of Trans World Airlines (TWA). The Trimotor was sold to Guinea Airways in December 1938. (DHM.)

Northern California aviator Kenneth Kleaver founded Kleaver Air Lines in the mid-1930s after purchasing a Fokker F-14 trimotor for $92,000. The airplane visited Bend on several occasions in the 1930s. This photograph was likely taken in the mid-1930s when Kleaver flew barnstorming tours throughout the Pacific Northwest. Prior to his 1936 Central Oregon visit, Kleaver had flown his ship in the Warner Brothers movie *China Clipper*. (Kleaver family.)

Registered as NC-27W, this Eyerly Coupe was built in Salem sometime between 1926 and 1934 by mechanic and inventor Lee Eyerly. The pilot was seated just aft of the wing in an open-air cockpit, while the passengers traveled in comfort in the enclosed cabin. In 1930, Eyerly founded Eyerly Aircraft Company to build two low-cost pilot trainers, the Whiffle Hen and the Orientator, a ground-based flight simulator. (DHM.)

This Whiffle Hen was owned by Harold Wagner. The airplane was built during the Great Depression to give pilots an opportunity to purchase their own aircraft. With the economic downturn, few people could afford luxury items such as airplanes. Highly affordable, the Whiffle Hen's engine burned only two gallons of fuel per hour. Eyerly was inducted into the Oregon Aviation Hall of Fame in 2001. (DHM.)

The Curtiss Wright Robin C-1 could accommodate two passengers. Priced at $7,500, the premiere flight took place in August 1928. A modified Robin piloted by Dale Jackson and Forest O'Brien stayed aloft for 17 days, 12 hours, and 17 minutes during a record-setting endurance flight at St. Louis, Missouri, in July 1929. The plane was kept airborne thanks to a crude air-to-air refueling system. (DHM.)

This Fleet Model 2, a two-seat primary trainer, was built by Fleet Aircraft in Canada. Between 1929 and 1939, over 200 Model 2s with a Kinner K-5 radial engine were built in the United States for the civilian market. Pictured from left to right to the right of the wing are Redmond aviation enthusiast J.R. Roberts, pilot and owner Art Whittaker, and former Oregon senator and Bend resident Jay Upton. (DHM.)

Redmond Motor Company mechanic Selby Towner purchased this Curtiss-Wright Jr. in late 1933. The plane was delivered from Reno, Nevada, to Lakeview, Oregon. In mid-December, Towner, together with pilot Ted Barber, flew the monoplane from Lakeview to Bend for final delivery to the Redmond Airport. Pictured from left to right are Selby Towner, Bill ?, Ted Barber, and Ray Glassow. (DHM.)

This Cessna DC-6A Chief was registered to Ray Wilson Inc. Aerial Photo Service and is pictured at Redmond's American Legion Airport. Equipped with a 300-horsepower Wright R-975 Whirlwind engine, the airplane was described as a four-seat touring plane. Due to the stock market crash in 1929, which diminished the demand for private aircraft, only about 20 of these airplanes were built. (DHM.)

Aeronautical Corporation of America, or Aeronca, was founded in Cincinnati, Ohio, in 1928. The company produced general aviation airplanes and later planes for the US armed forces. The Aeronca Model K Scout was first marketed in 1937, and more than 350 of the K version were built. This Aeronca KCA two-seater is equipped with a Continental A-50-1 engine. (DHM.)

Air tourism increased as the Great Depression subsided in the late 1930s. Pictured at Redmond Airport, these two Wacos flew in from Seattle, Washington. According to the information supplied with the photograph, pilots and passengers are, from left to right, Mr. and Mrs. Smith, Mr. and Mrs. Williamson, and Mr. Merrill. (DHM.)

The US Army Air Corps visited the Bend and Redmond airfields frequently. Here is a group of O-19 observation airplanes lined up at the Redmond Airport. The Ithaca, New York–based Thomas-Morse Aircraft Company produced 176 O-19 aircraft, which were used by both the US and Philippine armies. The two-seater featured an all-metal body and fabric-covered wings and tail surfaces. (DHM.)

Melvin "Mel" O'Day purchased his Eaglerock biplane from Eddie Campbell in Prineville in May 1937. The open, three-seat airplane was produced by Alexander Aircraft Company of Colorado Springs, Colorado. The Eaglerock was produced in the 1920s to replace the dwindling supply of World War I surplus aircraft such as the Curtiss JN-4. O'Day is standing over the engine while Cal Butler is on the ground by the propeller. (DHM.)

Five

REDMOND TAKES THE LEAD

A new player provided needed support to Central Oregon aviation both in Bend and Redmond. Founded after World War I, the American Legion took an active interest in furthering the development of local airports. Members of Redmond's Ray Jackson Post 44 and the Percy A. Stevens Post 4 in Bend helped develop airfields in both cities.

In 1928, the Redmond post purchased land on the east side of the Dalles-California Highway, a stone's throw from the original landing field at the Deschutes County Fairgrounds.

Redmond was not the only city in Central Oregon with plans for an airport. Perhaps still reeling from the loss of the fairgrounds to Redmond, Bend officials were not enthusiastic about Redmond's plan to build its own airfield.

In an interview conducted by Don Ellis in 1977 with Redmond businessman Porter "Mack" Houk, who was heavily involved with development of Redmond's airport, Houk said, "We had quite a battle with Bend. Bend city commissioners and county commissioners wanted to put an airport between Bend and Redmond."

The City of Bend eventually purchased a tract of land from E.H. Brandenburg north of Bend, near the Tumalo-Deschutes Road exit east of the Dalles-California Highway.

However, according to Houk, the newly acquired property had a flaw.

"When the airport people came out and inspected it, they found that hill out there was solid rock, and it would cost so much to [fix] it."

"[The airport people] said, why don't you go down and join Redmond in their airport," said Houk. "[But Bend officials] couldn't see it that way."

In November 1938, the editor for *The Redmond Spokesman* ran an editorial called "Footnote on Foresight." "Except for an occasional locally owned plane, and for a rare landing now and then of outside planes, Redmond Airport is as useless as a plat of flypaper at the North Pole."

Despite the negative introduction, the article provided a positive note on the foresight of Houk and J.R. Roberts, three-time mayor of Redmond: "If present uselessness is any criterion, the airport represents a staggering quantity of foresight."

After more than six years of work on the American Legion–supported Redmond Airport, the project gained assistance from the State Emergency Relief Administration in 1934. It was another two years before the federal Works Progress Administration (WPA) allotted additional funds. Pictured is J.R. Roberts surrounded by city officials and WPA workers. (DHM.)

Throughout the 1930s, work on the Redmond Airport progressed at a slow pace, in part due to the Great Depression. Although the economic downturn put pressure on many large projects, visionaries like J.R. Roberts, Mack Houk, and other residents never lost sight of the end goal: to create an aviation hub. From left to right are Warren F. "Jack" Hardison; Mary Brown, co-owner of *The Redmond Spokesman*; and J.R. Roberts. (DHM.)

Once the WPA put the airport project on its schedule, work moved faster. In an interview, Mack Houk explained how J.R. Roberts ended up being photographed driving a bulldozer: "He'd run it but took just a little jump and then he killed the engine, but it showed him and the WPA of the Roosevelt administration working on [the airport]." (DHM.)

The Redmond Airport slowly gained acceptance, and several aviators were based out of the landing field. In an early August 1937 article in *The Redmond Spokesman*, the writer noted, "Redmond now has three airplanes." The latest addition to the inventory was Roy Olsen's Golden Eagle monoplane in addition to Mel O'Day's Alexander Eaglerock. Selby Towner sold his Curtiss-Wright Jr. in 1937 and purchased the Taylor Cub pictured here. (DHM.)

Arthur "Art" Tift was appointed Redmond postmaster in 1925, a position held until his retirement in 1955. He oversaw the conversion to airmail during his 30-year tenure. The first trial runs with mail planes began sporadically arriving in Central Oregon in the early 1920s. Redmond's first airmail service began in 1928. Here, Tift (left) is greeted by Dr. Waco. (DHM.)

OREGON AIRWAYS

"SAVE A DAY EACH WAY"

PORTLAND TERMINAL — SWAN ISLAND AIRPORT

DAILY FLIGHT SCHEDULE

SOUTH BOUND		NORTH BOUND	
Lv. **PORTLAND** 10:00 A.M.		Lv. **COOS BAY** 3:00 P.M.	
Arr. **SALEM** 10:35 A.M.		Arr. **EUGENE** 3:55 P.M.	
Arr. **ALBANY** 10:45 A.M.		Arr. **ALBANY** 4:25 P.M.	
Arr. **EUGENE** 11:15 A.M.		Arr. **SALEM** 4:40 P.M.	
Arr. **COOS BAY** 12:15 P.M.		Arr. **PORTLAND** 5:15 P.M.	

SUBJECT TO WEATHER

Above Schedule Subject to Change Without Notice

NOTE—OREGON AIRWAYS PLANES CONNECT WITH UNITED AND NORTHWEST AIR LINES AT PORTLAND TO ALL POINTS NORTH — SOUTH — EAST

MAIL — EXPRESS

PRESENT LOW RATES PER PASSENGER

BETWEEN	ONE WAY	R. T.
PORTLAND—SALEM	$ 2.50	$ 4.55
PORTLAND—ALBANY	3.65	6.60
PORTLAND—EUGENE	6.60	11.85
PORTLAND—MARSHFIELD	10.90	19.65
SALEM—EUGENE	4.20	7.55
SALEM—MARSHFIELD	8.40	15.10
ALBANY—EUGENE	2.50	4.55
ALBANY—MARSHFIELD	6.70	12.10
EUGENE—MARSHFIELD	4.20	7.55

BAGGAGE UP TO 40 POUNDS CARRIED FREE

EXPRESS PACKAGE RATE

$1.00 up to 2 pounds — 8c additional for each pound over 2 pounds.

AS A SPECIAL COURTESY

You may leave your Stamped Air Mail with _____ We will carry it to Portland free of charge and mail it for you there, direct to air lines East, North and South, immediately upon our arrival in Portland.

OREGON AIRWAYS

FOR TICKETS AND INFORMATION PHONE

Portland Tr. 0859   Salem 6561   Albany 602J

Eugene 3272   Marshfield 57   North Bend 1001

Oregon Airways was a well-established airline, flying scheduled flights on the west side of the Cascades, when it approached Redmond officials to utilize their airport as part of its expanded service. In February 1940, owner Harry Stearns declared, "There can be only one main commercial landing field in Central Oregon. That field will be Redmond Airport. There is no other choice." (J.R. Roberts.)

In early 1940, Oregon Airways was vying for airline schedules and mail contracts from Portland to Klamath Falls via Central Oregon. At a meeting in Redmond in mid-February, O.O. Hagedorn and Asa Battles of the Prineville Chamber of Commerce gave their full support for developing a regional airport in Redmond. Alden Williams, who operated a flying school in Bend, explained, "I would like to see a large airport developed in Central Oregon." The Redmond Chamber of Commerce aviation committee was fully behind Oregon Airways' efforts, and in a show of support, Roberts signed on to fly to Washington, DC, to attend the Civil Aeronautics Authority hearing on September 31, 1940. Pictured above from left to right are Harry Stearns, J.R. Roberts, Tony Hinman, Edith Stearns, and Dave Lewis. Below is Governor Payne. (Both, J.R. Roberts.)

Roberts lobbied officials in Washington, DC, to support the airport in Redmond. Oregon senator Charles McNary was well known for his support of the Oregon lumber industry, but less clear was his interest in aviation. McNary introduced the Merchant Airship Bill in April 1930 to defray costs of building Goodyear-Zeppelin airships, a bill he later squashed after being lobbied by Pan American World Airways president Juan Trippe. (Library of Congress.)

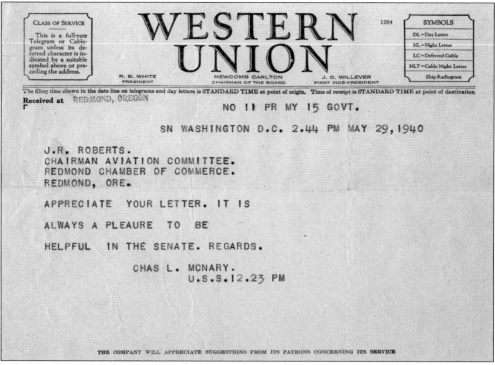

Roberts, chairman of the Redmond Chamber of Commerce aviation committee, and Senator McNary had a good working relationship. In what seems to have been a major turning point in the development of the Redmond Airport, Roberts lent his support to Oregon Airways, which was battling United Air Lines in its attempt to block the Portland-based airline from flying to Redmond. (J.R. Roberts.)

WESTERN UNION

1201

R. B. WHITE
PRESIDENT

NEWCOMB CARLTON
CHAIRMAN OF THE BOARD

J. C. WILLEVER
FIRST VICE-PRESIDENT

The filing time shown in the date line on telegrams and day letters is STANDARD TIME at point of origin. Time of receipt is STANDARD TIME at point of destination

CA79 42 NT 1 EXTRA =REDMOND ORG 25

J R ROBERTS =

WILLARD HOTEL WASHDC =

LEAVE NO STONE UNTURNED TO SECURE FRANCHISE FOR OREGON
AIRWAYS WE FEEL THAT IF THOSE PEOPLE DO NOT GET FRANCHISE
NO OTHER COMPANY WILL BE ABLE TO BENEFIT US. IF WE CAN
BE OF ANY FURTHER HELP WIRE US. BEST WISHES=

L E GARRISON   SECRETARY   REDMOND CHAMBER OF COMMERCE.

THE COMPANY WILL APPRECIATE SUGGESTIONS FROM ITS PATRONS CONCERNING ITS SERVICE

According to *The Redmond Spokesman* of October 3, 1940, the Civil Aeronautics Administration's decision would come down to the following: "If Oregon Airways wins, Central Oregon will get air service. If United wins, the service will go west of the mountains." Redmond Chamber of Commerce secretary L.E. Garrison wired Roberts while he was in Washington, telling him to "leave no stone unturned to secure franchise for Oregon Airways." (J.R. Roberts.)

After the Oregon Airways presentation in February, Roberts did not mince his words. Just because Redmond was the hands-down favorite for getting an air terminal, he said, "doesn't mean that all the Redmond Chamber of Commerce has to do now is to sit back and look pleased." In essence, Roberts was saying, "Now comes the real work." (DHM.)

The headline on the front page of *The Redmond Spokesman*'s February 13, 1941, edition said it all: "Roosevelt Slaps OK on Airport." The article described how Roberts, "his hat jammed down over his ears, emerged from his store shortly after 2 p.m. today, waving a telegram from Senator McNary. 'This looks very much like IT.'" It is worth noting that the approval for $717,000 was made 10 months shy of the United States' entrance into World War II. Oregon City–based Babler Bros. won the contract for construction of the airfield, which included two runways, administration buildings, and hangars. In honor of J.R. Roberts's tireless work to establish the Redmond Airport, it was officially christened Roberts Field on June 10, 1941. Taken by a US Army Air Force photographer, the photograph below shows the finished airport in 1941. (Above, DHM; below, US Army.)

Six

WORLD WAR II AVIATION IN CENTRAL OREGON

World War II broke out on September 1, 1939, when German military forces attacked Poland. Despite the terms stipulated by the 1919 Treaty of Versailles, which ended World War I, Germany had developed a strong mechanized military. As the world watched in horror, blitzkrieg ("lightning war") became a dreaded word.

In part thanks to President Wilson and his successors, the US armed forces were seriously underpowered compared with those of Germany and Japan. The development of airplanes, tanks, and other weapons had been basically at a standstill since World War I. The US Army was woefully unprepared for war.

The US Army Air Corps had few pilots. As World War II intensified in the early 1940s, local airfields around the nation were requisitioned by the Army for training fighter and bomber pilots. On June 25, 1942, *The Redmond Spokesman* announced that the Redmond city council had leased Roberts Field to the US government. The lease was effective as of June 1, 1942, and would run for the duration of the "existing wars in which the government is involved." The lease agreement also stated that the property would be turned back to the city within six months of the end of hostilities. The government would pay the city $1 a year for the lease.

Local contractor Warren Northwest was still in the process of finishing Runway "A" on July 25, 1942. At the same time, Babler Brothers graded and filled runways and taxiways, while Bend contractor Fred Van Matre worked on 22 wells to mitigate drainage from both runways.

Although Redmond's population was kept in the dark about the work at Roberts Field, Lt. Col. Earl Vance, base commander of the Walla Walla Army Air Base in Washington, opened the airfield for a public inspection on Sunday, July 26, 1942. The open house drew nearly 1,500 visitors.

Known as Army Air Base, Redmond, Oregon, it became home to the Second Air Force in December 1942, with Maj. Morell Brewster serving as the first of many commanding officers.

U.S.A. Leases Roberts Field For War Use

Council Authorizes Agreement Tuesday; Renewal Included

Execution of a lease to the United States of America on Roberts air field, Redmond municipal airport, was authorized Tuesday night by the city council. Unanimous roll call vote gave Mayor W. F. Hardison power to enter into the lease, requested by the government.

The lease includes all facilities and existing utility installations on the field, and right of ingress and egress over all existing roadways and rights of way in and from the field, and becomes effective as of June 1, 1942, ending June 30, 1943. Nominal rent of a dollar a year will be paid.

The Redmond Spokesman announced the agreement between the City of Redmond and the US Army on Thursday, June 25, 1942. One of the deciding factors for locating air bases in Central Oregon was favorable flying conditions. Mary Brown, co-publisher of the local newspaper and an avid aviatrix, later described the weather around Redmond in the March 1949 edition of *Flying*: "In summer the air is rough in the afternoon, with winds apt to be gusty, but normally very smooth in the early mornings and evening hours. Fall weather here is usually perfect, at least during September and most of October. In the spring, there is considerable wind, but hardly ever a day when one can't fly in the morning." Below is an aerial photograph of Redmond Army Air Base with completed A and B runways. The air base's Lockheed P-38s are lined up on the tarmac. (Both, DHM.)

Central Oregon residents became used to military aircraft crisscrossing the skies. On occasion, concerned citizens wrote letters to the editor about "buzzing" warplanes. Bend Airport manager Frank Stratton answered a February 1942 editorial in *The Bend Bulletin*, "The management of the Bend Airport regrets that citizens of Bend were disturbed and inconvenienced by the maneuvers but wishes to state we have no jurisdiction over army planes and pilots." (DHM.)

Invented by Ed Link in 1929, the Link trainer is considered the world's first flight simulator. The device was operated by an electric pump that could simulate pitch and roll as the pilot worked the primitive controls. The air base in Redmond received its first Link trainers in January 1943. This photograph shows a Link trainer at Freeman Field in Seymour, Indiana. (US Army.)

The air base went through its fair share of commanding officers. Maj. Morell Brewster took command in December 1942, followed by Capt. Eino Lahti (April–July 1943), 1st Lt. Marion Killian (temporary assignment), Capt. Mark Roach (July–December 1943), Lt. Col. Milton Kincaid (January–March 1944), Maj. Eugene Smith (March–April 1944), Capt. Harry Naumann (April–May 1944), Maj. Russell Vincent (May–December 1944, pictured), and Maj. Vinton Luther (January 1945 to the end of the war). (DHM.)

Central Oregon became the scene of one of the largest US Army maneuvers during the war. Blue and Red forces fought simulated battles from mid-July 1943 through October 31, 1943. On several occasions, planes from local bases flew simulated attacks against the troops. Although the event involved more than 90,000 soldiers, only 11 casualties were reported. This photograph shows Redmond Air Base's P-38s with the Three Sisters in the background. (Library of Congress.)

The US Army Air Force trained fighter pilots at a newly established air base in Prineville. Among the many civilian flight instructors was Ralph Scroggin, a Lebanon, Oregon, businessman. Scroggin tried to join the Army Air Force after the Japanese attack on Pearl Harbor but was turned down due to his age. Not satisfied with the outcome, he applied for a position as a civilian flight instructor. Scroggin was accepted and moved to Prineville with his wife, Grace (below). In 1944, the base was sold back to the City of Prineville and Crook County for $250. Scroggin worked with Prineville officials to convert the airfield to a civilian airport. He founded the Prineville Flying Service and remained focused on his original mission, to teach civilians to fly. (Above, Prineville Crook County Airport; below, Bowman Museum.)

Although the formative steps to build an airport in Madras began in September 1934, when Jefferson County optioned 40 acres on the south end of Agency Plains, it took another five years before an airfield was constructed. After a push by the US Army to build additional training fields in Central Oregon, crews from Morris-Knudsen Construction Company began building the airfield in early 1943. (Jefferson County Historical Society.)

The budget for constructing a 7,400-foot runway with taxiways was in excess of a million dollars. The hangars built to house B-17 Flying Fortresses (visible to the left of the flagpole), were also finished. In January 1943, Maj. Joseph Arnold, brother to Lt. Gen. "Hap" Arnold, was appointed the commanding officer of Madras Army Airfield. (Jefferson County Historical Society.)

The Army airfield went through major changes in February 1944, when the Second Air Force was succeeded by the Fourth Air Force. The focus shifted from training B-17 pilots to fly battle formations to training fighter pilots. The base became home to the 546th Fighter Squadron of the 475th Fighter Group and their P-39Q Airacobras (pictured) and P-63 King Cobras. (US Air Force.)

The United Service Organization's Madras location provided a home away from home for the men stationed at the air base. The mission of the Madras base changed again in September 1944 to airplane maintenance with only a skeleton crew on hand. The base was declared military surplus in November 1945, and on April 3, 1947, ownership reverted to Madras and Jefferson County. (Jefferson County Historical Society.)

World War II fighter pilot Lt. Rex T. Barber had a date with destiny on April 18, 1943, when he and 15 other Lockheed P-38 pilots set out on a top-secret mission over the northern Solomon Islands in Japanese-controlled airspace. Skimming above the water to avoid detection, the aircraft intercepted Adm. Isoruko Yamamoto's "Betty" bomber and shot down the aircraft carrying the architect of the Pearl Harbor attack. After the raid, Capt. Thomas Lamphier (left above) claimed that he alone had downed Yamamoto's plane. Barber (right) also claimed the prize and for 48 years the US Air Force debated the controversy. As of 1991, when the Air Force made its final decision, they share the "kill." Below are two Lockheed P-38 Lightnings. (Above, National Air & Space Museum; below, DHM.)

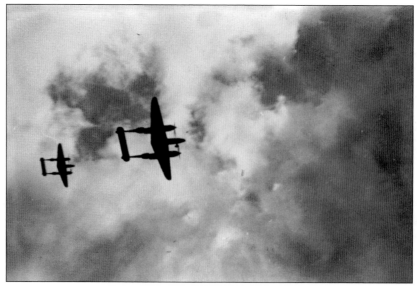

At the end of the war, Barber attained the rank of major and later commanded one of America's first jet squadrons. He retired from the Air Force in 1961 as a colonel and eventually returned to Terrebonne, Oregon. Continuing in his parents' footsteps, he operated a farm in Terrebonne while working as an insurance agent. Barber also became the mayor of Culver. (Author's collection.)

In honor of Barber's service to his country, the newly constructed bridge spanning the Crooked River gorge was renamed the Rex T. Barber Veterans Memorial Bridge in 2003. Additionally, US Highway 97 was designated the World War II Veterans Historic Highway in May 2009. (Library of Congress.)

Bend aviatrix Helen Skjersaa was one of only 1,074 pilots accepted into the Women Airforce Service Pilots corps, or WASPs. "Ever since she was a little girl, mom always looked skywards. She wanted to fly," said her daughter Genevieve Haugh in a 2016 interview. In September 1939, Helen left Bend for the University of Idaho, one of many educational centers across the United States with an aeronautics curriculum. (Bill Mayer.)

By the time she applied to WASP, Skjersaa had three years of college and 200 hours of flying time to her credit. Even though the average applicant had about 1,000 flying hours in their logbook, Skjersaa was considered accomplished enough to be accepted into the program. On December 17, 1943, she became a member of the ferrying command, flying B-17s, B-24s, and B-25s. She is pictured here with her brother Norman (left) and an unidentified aviator. (Bill Mayer.)

Model airplane clubs sprang up all over the United States in the late 1930s. According to Phil Peoples, his father, Ray, gave him a five-foot model plane kit in the summer of 1939—the start of a long career in aeronautics. Phil (far right) joined the Bend Model Flying Club. Headquartered at the Bend Drake Park bandstand, where this photograph was taken in 1940, model airplane competitions were held on the dry lake bed at the old Tumalo Reservoir. (Laura Goetz.)

As the United States was pulled into the war, Phil Peoples and his brother Sam joined the US Army Air Force. Phil flew P-47s with the 12th Air Force and Sam flew P-51s with the 15th Air Force. In March 1945, Phil visited Sam's base in Fano, Italy. Sam (left) and Phil are pictured in front of Phil's plane *Bend er Bust*. After the war, both brothers worked for the Boeing Company in Seattle. (Laura Goetz.)

Leon Devereaux Jr. credits his father for his interest in aviation. In the early 1930s, Leon Sr. and his son flew in a visiting Ford Trimotor. "I remember sitting on bamboo chairs on my dad's lap," said Devereaux in a June 2020 interview. The 20-minute ride made Leon an aviation enthusiast. Attending Oregon State University, he was recruited by the US Navy in March 1943, completed flight training, and was commissioned an ensign on July 14, 1944. (Leon Devereaux Jr.)

Flying F-4U Corsairs off the aircraft carrier USS *Shangri-La*, Ensign Devereaux downed a Japanese "Betty" bomber over Hokkaido in July 1945. He was also one of many who joined the air armada flying over the battleship USS *Missouri* in Tokyo Bay during the signing of the peace treaty with Japan. Devereaux returned to Bend and was elected mayor in 1968 (third from left). (DHM.)

Calvin J. Butler graduated from Union High School in Redmond in 1937. Like many teenagers at the time, Butler was looking skyward, learning to fly at Redmond Airport. Not able to afford the $5 an hour lessons, he instead bought 15-minute sessions. He joined the US Army Air Corps in September 1940 and completed his final 10 weeks of advanced flying at Moffett Field in California. (DHM.)

Butler was commissioned a second lieutenant in June 1941. He was sent to Europe, flying P-38 support missions for the B-17 armadas on bombing runs over German-controlled airspace. On June 17, 1944, his luck ran out over France and he spent the rest of the war as a POW. After the war, Butler returned to Redmond and started his own crop-dusting company, Butler Farm Air Company. (June Butler Jaeger.)

Adventurous to a fault, Redmond youth Everett "Jigger" Endicott decided to get a pilot's license in 1939. However, he could not get on the list at the Civilian Pilot Training Program (CPTP) at Redmond Airport. "Ernie Sink, who ran the program, told me he'd give me a private license if I could come up with the money," he said. Determined, Endicott borrowed the money, and after eight hours of flying with an instructor, he soloed. (Endicott family.)

At age 22, Endicott enlisted in the Army Air Corps. After receiving his wings, he put in a request to fly single-engine fighters. However, while the rest of his class was sent overseas, Endicott was told to stay behind as a flight instructor. After the war, he got a job flying crop-dusters for Cal Butler. "I was doing well until I tried to cut down a juniper tree in Prineville," he said. (Bowman Museum.)

Frank Stratton learned to fly from Bend flight instructor Alden Williams. Stratton received his pilot license in April 1939 at the age of 34. A year later, he became the airport manager for Bend, as well as a flight instructor for the CPTP. Stratton was also a certified engine mechanic, the only one in Central Oregon. (Prineville Crook County Airport.)

In September 1942, Stratton and the Tilse Flying Service moved into a new administration and classroom building at Bend Airport. Surrounded by students, Stratton, third from left, left Bend for Tex Rankin Aeronautic Academy in Tulare, California, to become an instructor. After the war, he relocated to Prineville Airport, where he operated a small airline. (Prineville Crook County Airport.)

With the US Army taking control of the Redmond airfield, city officials began looking for an alternative. According to Houk, they found a flat property at Cline Falls: "[We] went out there with our city graders and had another Airport Day. The [residents] went out and pulled all the trees, sagebrush, and junipers." The quick turnaround became known as "An Airport in a Day." The September 3, 1944, edition of the *Sunday Oregonian* reported, "The field was a sagebrush flat in the morning. At 4 P.M. a plane landed." The first airplane to land was piloted by Lt. Walter Howard, commander of the Bend Civil Air Patrol (CAP) squadron. Below is moving day from Cline Falls airfield to Redmond Airport in 1946. From left to right are Bob Ballantine, J.R. Roberts, Mary Brown, Ted Wells, two unidentified, and Warren Hardison. (Both, DHM.)

Although ownership of the Army airfield at Redmond did not revert to the City of Redmond until mid-1946, an interim permit to use the airfield was granted in late February 1946. With a stroke of a pen, the Army airfield became Roberts Field once more. The vastly improved airfield was a welcomed sight for city officials and pilots alike. Even with much work done by the US Army Air Corps, the Redmond Airport was still considered a Class 5 airport. The first plane to land at the Redmond Airport was Maj. T.J. Wells's Fairchild PT-23 with J.R. Roberts in the passenger seat. Pictured at right sitting on the wing is J.R. Roberts. Below, from left to right, are Dick Ballantine, T.J. Wells, Warren Hardison, Jim Short, unidentified, J.R. Roberts, Mary Brown, and unidentified. (J.R. Roberts.)

At the end of World War II, the Civil Aeronautics Administration (CAA) began planning for peacetime development of the nation's airports. In December 1944, the CAA presented Congress with an airport master plan, which included Redmond (above). In anticipation of the end of the lease, Redmond City Council started feasibility studies regarding operating the former air base as a municipal airport. In October 1945, the city council approved the formation of the Airport Committee. It included J.R. Roberts, T.J. Wells, Jim Short, Forrest Cooper, and Warren Hardison. The World War II hangar below was a familiar landmark until December 30, 1969, when it was destroyed in a fire. Seven airplanes were lost. Thanks to the efforts of bystanders, an old B-17 Flying Fortress barely escaped the blaze. (Both, DHM.)

Seven

AIRLINES TAKE TO THE SKY

Throughout the war years, the US government changed its stance on who was going to pay for the development of airports. With millions of federal dollars invested in military airfield infrastructure, the government realized its investment could support a burgeoning civilian airline market.

In November 1945, Redmond's J.R. Roberts and director Leo Devaney of the Oregon State Board of Aeronautic traveled to St. Louis to attend a meeting arranged by the National Association of State Aviation Officials. The focus of the meeting was to discuss the future of aviation. One of the discussion points was local airfields under lease from the government. These were expected to be returned to local governments as soon as they were declared surplus.

The Redmond Army Airfield was put on the inactive list in mid-October 1945 and sold to Redmond for a dollar in 1946. Included in the purchase price were buildings, facilities, and maintenance equipment.

Bringing air service to Central Oregon was not without controversy. In mid-September 1945, Western Airlines was seeking approval before the Civilian Aeronautics Board (CAB) for approval to operate scheduled flights to Redmond as a part of its Seattle to San Francisco service.

At approximately the same time, United Air Lines (UAL) was making inroads to provide similar service through its Portland to Klamath Falls route. The request sat pending until May 1946, when the CAB approved UAL's application. The decision irked the Portland and Klamath Falls chambers of commerce, which both insisted on approving Western Airlines' application instead.

The request to CAB to reconsider the approval was based on the wish to promote healthy competition between West Coast air carriers. If a rehearing was approved, the chambers of Bend, The Dalles, and Klamath Falls feared the approval could delay air service by more than a year.

CAB's decision to allow UAL to serve Central Oregon withstood the challenge. The first scheduled flight was set for September 1, 1946. However, due to difficulties with hiring qualified staff at Redmond Airport, the airline pushed back the inaugural flight to October 3.

Announcing Commercial
AIR SERVICE
For Central Oregon
Starting Monday, Dec. 3

OREGON AIR LINES
Flight Schedules
Portland - Eugene - Redmond

Air Lines Comes to Central Oregon

REDMOND RESERVATION OFFICE
435 Sixth Street   Phone 235
BEND RESERVATION OFFICE
Pilot Butte Inn   Phone 123
E. L. WOODARD, Central Oregon Representative

The first daily commercial air service to Central Oregon after the war was provided by Oregon Air Lines. Using a twin-engine Cessna, the airline flew the Redmond-to-Portland route out of Troutdale Airport. At the time of the inaugural flight on December 3, 1945, ownership of Roberts Field had not yet reverted to the City of Redmond. Instead, Oregon Air Lines used the airport at Cline Falls. Pictured from left to right are R.A. Alexander of Western Skyways; Dick Ballantine; Warren Hardison of Redmond Airport Commission; Harry Siegrist, pilot (standing on the wing); Warren Ward, Oregon Air Lines manager; Lester Houk, Redmond Chamber of Commerce president; J.R. Roberts, member of the airport commission and the Oregon State Board of Aeronautics; Dr. Hal Rogers; Maurice Robert, commanding officer of the Redmond CAP; and Redmond businessman "Mack" Houk. (*The Redmond Spokesman.*)

One unmistakable clue that Roberts Field was about to gain official status was the establishment of a CAA area office in Redmond on February 21, 1946. A week later, the Army engineers in Portland received authority to grant the City of Redmond interim permission to utilize Roberts Field. The airfield featured two paved 7,000-foot runways as well as taxiways, parking aprons, hangars, and other buildings. (DHM.)

Throughout July 1946, UAL's DC-3 Mainliner made daily landings and take-offs at Roberts Field in preparation for regularly scheduled flights to and from Central Oregon. In a peculiar twist, the CAA authorized UAL to operate from the Bend Airport. However, to fulfill the agreement with CAA, Bend Airport first had to be developed to handle heavy commercial aircraft, which never came to fruition. (DHM.)

The establishment of a national airline at Redmond Airport was big news during the summer of 1946. Planning for the inaugural flight began in mid-September in cooperation between Redmond and Bend officials. The theme of the celebration was "transportation from the stone age to the present." Central Oregon Air Transport Day was celebrated on October 3, 1946, when UAL's Mainliner 180 touched down at Roberts Field at 9:53 a.m. (DHM.)

The Mainliner was piloted by captain Dick Appleby and first flight officer Russ Hopkins. Appleby radioed the airport during the final approach so people could hear him over the loudspeakers. Leaving Redmond, Bend and Redmond mayors A.T. Niebergall and Maurice Roberts sent gifts to the mayors of Portland, Seattle, San Francisco, and Los Angeles. Included were boxes of Central Oregon strawberries, Deschutes Netted Gem potatoes, and letters from the mayors. (J.R. Roberts.)

Among the invited guests was 90-year-old Ida Kennard (right). She and her husband, Fred, came to Redmond in 1906. She became the first telephone operator in Redmond and attended Railroad Day on July 4, 1911. Thirty-five years later, she returned to Redmond to experience the next phase of mass transportation and visit her granddaughter Patt Kennard (second from right), who was a stewardess for UAL in Seattle. (J.R. Roberts.)

Before the southbound Mainliner departed, a Parade of Transportation was featured to show how Central Oregon had developed over the years. Leading the parade was Slim Talbot representing Pony Express riders, followed by a pack string loaded with mail, a horse and buggy, and a modern bus. The program also included a safe-flying show with Dick Ballantine, Ollie Bowman of Tilse Bowman Flying Services, and Frank Stratton, manager of Prineville Airport. (DHM.)

United Air Lines operated their DC-3s under the Mainliner 180 moniker. The California-based Douglas Aircraft Company began development of the revolutionary new plane in 1935. Originally designed to hold 14 to 16 sleeping berths, a requirement made by American Airlines CEO C.R. Smith, another version was equipped with 21 seats. The two Wright R-1820 Cyclone engines gave the DC-3 a cruising speed of 207 mph, able to fly from New York to Los Angeles in 18 hours with three refueling stops. The first commercial DC-3 flight took place on June 26, 1936, flying American Airlines colors. During World War II, the DC-3 was called into action as the C-47 Skytrain or Dakota. After the war, surplus military C-47s flooded the market and American air carriers converted them back to civilian airliners. (Above, DHM; below, J.R. Roberts.)

United Air Lines was created by mergers of several airlines and aviation-related businesses in the late 1920s and early 1930s, with William Boeing's Boeing Air Transport and Pratt & Whitney Aircraft being the nucleus. During a 28-month buying spree, the company purchased Varney Airlines of Boise, Idaho; Pacific Air Transport, Oregon; Stout Air Services, Dearborn, Michigan; and National Air Transport, operating at Chicago Municipal Airport. The different subsidiaries were organized under the name United Air Lines. At the time of the inaugural flight to Central Oregon, the airline was expanding its route network. Not attending the October 3 event, UAL president William "Pat" Patterson visited Redmond on October 14, 1946. Arriving in the Mainliner *Oregon*, Patterson was greeted by Redmond, Bend, and Prineville dignitaries. Below, from left to right are J.R. Roberts, Redmond mayor Maurice Roberts, and Patterson. (Both, J.R. Roberts.)

In preparation for UAL's arrival in Redmond, assistant plant engineer George Marschino made arrangements for the construction of a 20-by-45-foot steel structure to function as the local field office. Parts for the temporary office began arriving in early August 1946, and the building was still under construction in late September, only days before the inaugural flight. The building featured an office and a small waiting room. (Bowman Museum.)

Save Time—in
United Mainliners

PORTLAND	1¼ hrs.	$ 5.80
SEATTLE	2⅔ hrs.	12.05
SAN FRANCISCO	4 hrs.	18.50
LOS ANGELES	6½ hrs.	33.65

and "all the East." All fares, tax extra.

For reservations:
Bend-Redmond Airport Redmond 260

UNITED AIR LINES

SHIP BY AIR FREIGHT

THE MAIN LINE AIRWAY

This ad for United Air Lines was published in *The Redmond Spokesman* on March 13, 1947. Today, one can fly from Redmond to Portland in about 45 minutes, compared with the one-hour-and-fifteen-minute hop on the Mainliner. It was a huge timesaver, though, considering a trip to Portland by train was a day-long affair. The $5.80 one-way airline ticket, however, is considerably more expensive today. (DHM.)

During the prewar era, Redmond officials marketed the city as "the Hub." According to local newspaper advertising, Redmond was strategically located in the middle of an intersection of different transportation modes. Whether coming or going, people in the area had access to the railroad as well as two major highways, US Routes 97 and 126, neatly tying together access to surrounding cities like Bend, Sisters, Madras, and Prineville. (J.R. Roberts.)

United Air Lines' West Coast passenger and mail service had a robust network on the west side of the Cascades. Its decision to make Central Oregon a part of UAL's network, with a daily route from Portland to Klamath Falls via Redmond, gave Central Oregonians access to the air carrier's over 60 US destinations. It also meant connections to cities all over the world. (J.R. Roberts.)

By 1950, Redmond Airport had outgrown its administration building, and the temporary United Air Lines office was outdated. Construction of a new station building began in March 1950. With a $22,000 grant from the CAA and additional money from the state aeronautics administration, the Redmond Airport Commission spent $17,200 on the construction, for a total cost of $40,000. In August of the same year, the new building was move-in ready. (Both, J.R. Roberts.)

A vast improvement compared to the old terminal, the new building featured downstairs office space for United Air Lines as well as upstairs offices for the CAA. The adjacent building to the left was the office of Tilse-Bowman Air Services, which at the time operated out of both Redmond and Bend Airports. (J.R. Roberts.)

At Dedication Day, a special tribute was paid to J.R. Roberts, "whose early-day efforts were largely responsible for the development of the pioneer Redmond field," according to a front-page article in *The Bend Bulletin*. Pictured in front of the new building are, from left to right, UAL Redmond station manager John Sedell, J.R. Roberts, and Seeley Hall, UAL general manager of ground services. (J.R. Roberts.)

The new building was dedicated on Sunday, September 17, 1950. Hundreds of people gathered in front of the building, reported *The Bend Bulletin*. One of UAL's DC-3s circled Roberts Field while the national anthem was piped out over the loudspeaker system. Between departing and arriving flights, dignitaries from local, state, and CAA offices addressed the crowd. An improvised speaker's stand is visible at left. (J.R. Roberts.)

This montage shows (from left to right) former Redmond resident and new state director of aeronautics Jack Bartlett, CAA region director Robert Bedinger, and Redmond mayor Marion Coyner at the dedication. Speaking to a gathering of spectators, "they traced the development of the Redmond Airport, which had its start as 'a runway from which rocks had been rolled aside,'" according to *The Bend Bulletin*. (J.R. Roberts.)

The overarching theme carried by many speakers was that Redmond Airport was not just a Redmond affair, but a regional asset. Coyner highlighted the role of the Redmond Airport Commission. "[It] assumed the full responsibility of making the Redmond 'air industry' a financial success [and] assumed the responsibility of developing a great asset, not only for Redmond but for all of Central Oregon." (J.R. Roberts.)

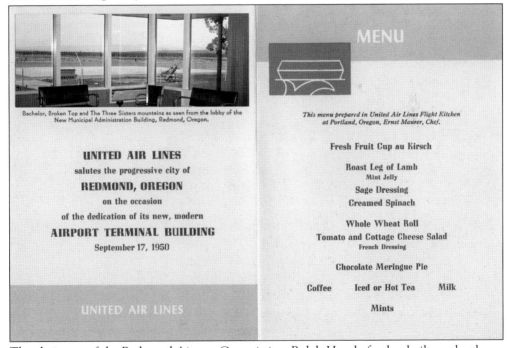

Bachelor, Broken Top and The Three Sisters mountains as seen from the lobby of the New Municipal Administration Building, Redmond, Oregon.

This menu prepared in United Air Lines Flight Kitchen at Portland, Oregon, Ernst Maurer, Chef.

UNITED AIR LINES

salutes the progressive city of

REDMOND, OREGON

on the occasion

of the dedication of its new, modern

AIRPORT TERMINAL BUILDING

September 17, 1950

UNITED AIR LINES

MENU

Fresh Fruit Cup au Kirsch

Roast Leg of Lamb
Mint Jelly
Sage Dressing
Creamed Spinach

Whole Wheat Roll
Tomato and Cottage Cheese Salad
French Dressing

Chocolate Meringue Pie

Coffee   Iced or Hot Tea   Milk

Mints

The chairman of the Redmond Airport Commission, Ralph Hauck, further built on the theme in his presentation, telling the audience that, "the new building and the big airport are not only serving Redmond, but the entire area." Invited guests were treated to a special meal prepared in UAL's flight kitchen in Portland by chef Ernst Maurer. (J.R. Roberts.)

Described in *The Bend Bulletin* on August 5, 1950, as a "Modernistic Structure," the newspaper reported, "The New Building at Redmond Airport Now Occupied." The result of the seven-month construction and improvement project was a far cry from the buildings left over from the US Army Air Corps. The newspaper also described the interior as having "soft decorator colors, pleasing to the eye." (DHM.)

Although more than 70 years have passed since the opening of the new administration building, many things have stayed the same. Transported back in time via these photographs, any airport passenger of today would feel comfortable at Roberts Field of the 1950s. Here is station agent Curt Simonson on the phone. (DHM.)

Station agent Floyd Miller is posted at the teletype machine. A similar machine was installed in the upstairs CAA office, which received hourly weather information from all over the United States and Canada. According to John Sedell, station manager (not pictured), UAL owned "10,500 miles of private telephone lines and a teletype circuit that carries 22,000 million words a day to 80 major cities," according to an August 5, 1950, article in *The Bend Bulletin*. (DHM.)

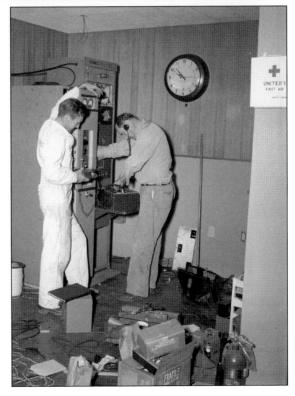

In preparation for the grand opening, a month away, United Air Lines ground communication technicians work on installing new radio equipment. Hard at work are C.J. Lingo of Denver, Colorado (left), and D.W. Press of Portland. (DHM.)

Oregon became the first state in the United States to create a government agency with the authority to develop and regulate the aviation industry. With the founding of the Oregon State Board of Aeronautics in 1921 by the Oregon legislature, the agency's mission included the oversight of pilots and aircraft. The board administered pilot examinations, which included all aspects of flying, from the theory of flight to mechanics. A pilot also had to show that he or she possessed moral and physical characteristics to safely operate an aircraft. Two years later, the state aeronautics board started assessing an annual registration fee of $10 per aircraft. The secretary of state, in turn, issued metal registration plates to be mounted on the airplane. Here is a photograph of the Oregon State Board of Aviation at Klamath Falls in the late 1950s. From left to right are Pat Maroney, Ben Ruffner, J.R. Roberts, Lee Eyerly, Doc Peare, Jack Bartlett, and Gen. Cart McCartney. (J.R. Roberts.)

Eight

GENERAL AVIATION
IN CENTRAL OREGON

As Roberts Field cemented its role as the main commercial air transportation hub in Central Oregon, many of the smaller airfields in the region developed into flourishing general aviation airports for private and corporate pilots.

Throughout World War II, the state and federal governments invested more than $4 million in Madras's airport and approximately $6,000 at Prineville. There is no evidence that Bend Airport received state or federal funding.

The City of Bend abandoned its Long Butte airport in the late 1930s and began looking for a third place to call home. In 1942, Bend eventually settled on a property close to the city along the Powell Butte Highway.

Though civil aviation was heavily restricted during the war, private pilots kept flying for the CAP and CPTP, two government-sponsored organizations with the mission to develop a new generation of pilots. Both programs ended up a success, with the US Army Air Corps and the US Navy taking pilots from the CPTP for further training. The CAP played an important role in the civil defense sector during the war. Local CAP pilots flew daily courier flights between military airfields in Central Oregon.

Shortly after the war, the Servicemen's Readjustment Act of 1944, also known as the GI Bill, was a catalyst to an explosive growth in general aviation. The "Golden Age of Civil Aviation" was underway, in part powered by the release of thousands of military aviators in addition to other veterans interested in earning a pilot's license under the GI Bill.

The three largest aircraft manufacturers—Cessna, Piper, and Beech—were doing brisk business fueled by an insatiable demand for aircraft. There was also an abundance of inexpensive surplus military airplanes.

In the early 1980s, several factors put a lid on the exploding general aviation market. Insurance rates skyrocketed for airplane manufacturers after million-dollar product liability lawsuits became the norm. There was also a glut of aircraft due to overproduction as well as a worsening recession. In addition, commercial airfares were dropping and fuel prices increasing.

Sisters's introduction to aviation took place in the late 1920s and early 1930s. As in other Central Oregon cities, the fairground had enough room for a landing strip. Early aviation had its ups and downs. In the early 1930s, schoolchildren were invited to the fair to see a real airplane fly. The pilot took off and crashed shortly afterward. No one was hurt. (Sisters Eagle Airport.)

It would take until 1935 to establish Sisters's first airport, when George Wakefield purchased the land north of the fairgrounds. With the help of US Forest Service employees and Civilian Conservation Corps workers, Wakefield carved out a small airstrip. In the early 1940s, Maurice Hitchcock (pictured), the "Flying Lumberman," purchased land next to the airfield plus the property where the landing field was located. (DHM.)

In the March 1949 edition of *Flying* magazine, the airfield was described as a "private field maintained by Mr. Hitchcock for his personal use." Although the magazine described the airfield as having no services available, it noted that "visiting planes are welcome." Hitchcock sold the ranch and airfield to Harold Barclay, who in turn donated it to the State of Oregon in 1967. After 1978, when the state lost interest in keeping up the airport, the property changed hands several times. Among the owners was Clifton Clemens, who operated the airport on a one-person basis. Today, Sisters Eagle Airport is owned by Benny and Julie Benson, who purchased it in 2011 after locating their company, Energyneering Solutions, there in 2008. The current master plan (below) includes a terminal building with a small restaurant. (Both, Sisters Eagle Airport.)

The Madras Army Airfield, as well as former military airfields in Salem and Medford, came under the custody of the War Assets Administration (WAA) in early February 1947. On April 3, the WAA turned over the air base to Jefferson County and Madras and advertised the sale of the leftover buildings. A total of 48 buildings were sold to local buyers. (Jefferson County Historical Society.)

The US Army spent over $4.1 million on constructing the bomber defense base, according to a February 26, 1947, article in *The Bend Bulletin*. What was left of the 2,069-acre base was divided between the City of Madras and a federal land bank. Madras kept 575 acres and 13 buildings, among them the giant hangars that housed the repair shops for the B-17s. Pictured are Vivian and Frank Stratton in front of one of the hangars. (Prineville Crook County Airport.)

The City-County Airport Commission was established on May 8, 1947. According to an interview with Redmond mayor George Endicott in 2019, J.R. Roberts talked Everett Endicott and Cal Butler into bidding on the contracts to operate the Redmond and Madras airports, which they did. As the story goes, the two men flipped a coin, making Endicott the operator of Madras Airport and Butler taking charge of Redmond Airport. (Jefferson County Historical Society.)

Operating under the name Jefferson Air Service, Endicott announced he would operate airplane servicing facilities as well as access to both 80- and 90-octane Shell aviation gasoline. In September 1947, Endicott signed a contract with the Veteran's Administration to operate a GI flight school at Madras Field, offering primary training to World War II veterans. Pictured here is downtown Madras. (DHM.)

The Erickson Aircraft Collection was founded by Jack Erickson in 1991 when he began displaying his prized aircraft in an old US Navy blimp hangar near Tillamook, Oregon. Among them were a P-51D Mustang, F4U Corsair, and a British Mark VIII Spitfire. In 2014, the collection was moved from Tillamook to Madras. With more than 20 World War II–era aircraft, many in flying condition, the collection has become a mecca for aviation enthusiasts. Among the airplanes displayed at the large hangar in Madras is a B-17 Flying Fortress, the *Madras Maiden*, the same type of airplane based at the Madras Army Airfield during World War II. Also displayed is a Grumman Ag Cat (below), perhaps a tip of the hat to Madras farmers who hired similar planes to crop-dust their fields. (Both, author's collection.)

Madras began an ambitious upgrade program of its municipal airport in early 2000, in part due to flourishing business at the Jefferson Park Business Center adjacent to the airport. The more than 50-year-old, 600-square-foot terminal building was replaced in 2004 with a modern office building. With the transfer of the Tillamook Air Museum to Madras, the need for a large hangar to house the collection became clear. It was completed in August 2014. Improvement projects have continued, including a four-month construction project in 2015 to completely rebuild the main 5,089-foot runway originally constructed in the 1940s. (Both, author's collection.)

Former Bend Airport manager Frank Stratton moved his business to Prineville in 1946. Operating as Frank Stratton Air Service, he continued Ralph Scroggin's work. An ad in the May 23, 1946, *Central Oregonian* announced that veterans eligible for flight training under the GI Bill could receive training through Stratton's flight school. Pictured here is Frank Stratton in front of a Stinson. (Prineville Crook County Airport.)

In the March 1949 issue of *Flying* magazine, Prineville was described as a "small commercial field [with] 80 octane gas and A&E service." Dick Ballantine, former Redmond CAP airfield manager, established Ballantine Flying Service in 1954. After receiving CAA approval in mid-1954, Ballentine advertised in the local Polk Directory, "Courses are open to all, including Korean War Vets under Public Law 550." (Prineville Crook County Airport.)

The Bend Bulletin published the first of a four-part series on local airports in November 1955. Crook County's airport got top billing: "Prineville Getting Air-Minded, Activity at Airport Indicates." According to airport manager Dick Ballantine, "Traveling salesmen and businessmen are more frequently saving time and making more money by flying. You can purchase a good used plane for about half the price of an automobile, and they are more economical to operate." Above is a Cessna T-50 light transport plane, also known as a "Bamboo Bomber." (Prineville Crook County Airport.)

Adapting to a mode of transportation that made it possible to cover great distances, pilot Rev. C.G. Herring of Cleveland, Tennessee–based Church of God of Prophecy operated a revival ministry in the mid-1950s. Together with fellow pilot and overseer Adolph Flemmer, the church maintained two airplanes at Prineville airport: a Stinson (pictured) and a Cessna. Both were used for missionary work around the Pacific Northwest. (Prineville Crook County Airport.)

The city of Prineville and its airport have enjoyed an economic lift during the first part of the 21st century. Improvement projects at the airport got underway in 2004 with the widening of the main runway, added taxiways, and improved lighting. Moving away from an old, leaky World War II–era terminal building, the new airport administration building was opened to the public in May 2008. (City of Prineville.)

Kelly Coffelt became airport manager in January 2012 and is credited with strengthening the position of Prineville Airport among general aviation pilots. In addition to adding hangar space, Coffelt has overseen several improvement projects. Among them are new US Forest Service facilities as well as an above-ground fueling facility on the north end of the airport. Facebook and Apple data centers are next-door neighbors to the airport. (Author's collection.)

The latest addition to the general aviation landscape in Central Oregon was the construction of Sunriver Airport in 1968. Originally conceived as a convenience to the developers of the Sunriver property, the paved runway was constructed almost at the same time construction of the Sunriver Lodge began. The price for the original airstrip was $197,000. (Sunriver Owners Association.)

The airport was inaugurated on August 11, 1968, with a "fly-in" by the Hillsboro chapter of the Oregon Pilot's Association. Today, more than 50 years later, Sunriver Airport is planning to replace the aging terminal with a new two-story building with a second-floor restaurant. Sunriver Airport manager Brandon Wright is also planning to build hangars to allow a maintenance company to repair aircraft at the airport. (Sunriver Owners Association.)

Maintaining a serene and relaxed atmosphere throughout the environmentally sensitive area, pilots using Sunriver's airport are urged to adhere to the resort's noise abatement rules. As visiting pilots can attest, the sign is gone, but the rule remains. Airport use is mainly general aviation; however, as much as 15 percent of the flights are companies flying their executives to Sunriver for vacations. (Sunriver Owners Association.)

The airport was originally managed by Sunriver Resort. Since 2018, it has been operated by Sunriver Airport LLC, a separate entity. The original airstrip was upgraded and expanded in 1985 to accommodate multi-engine and private jets, and in April 2009, it was widened and repaved to accommodate heavier aircraft. Since 2019, further improvements to the taxiway and ramp have taken place. (Sunriver Owners Association.)

Thanks to its central location, visitors to Sunriver have access to many of Central Oregon's tourist spots. Among these are Mount Bachelor Ski Area, Lava Lands Visitor Center, and Sunriver Resort with its abundance of attractions and scenic beauty. With the Cascade Mountains nearby, winter weather can affect flight operations at Sunriver Airport. At 4,163 feet elevation, storms can dump massive amounts of snow in a relatively short time. (Sunriver Owners Association.)

Sunriver Airport is one of the busier general aviation airports in Oregon. With Sunriver Airport LLC taking over management, the airport has invested in new fuel trucks and snowplows. Improvements also include the installation of an Automated Weather Observing System. Beyond general aviation and corporate traffic, the airport is also an important cog in the area's aerial firefighting capabilities. (Sunriver Owners Association.)

With increasing military spending on airports during World War II, Bend was vying for a flight school. Thomas Brooks, chairman of the chamber of commerce airport committee, pushed the city to finance a new municipal airport along Butler Market Road through a $25,000 bond issue, which the voters approved. Located on the Schanno and Fitzgerald properties as well as federal land, Bend inaugurated the airfield in June 1942. (Bend–Fort Rock District, Deschutes National Forest.)

Tilse Flying Service, owned by Al Tilse of Bend, received approval to train pilots under the Civilian Pilot Training Program in April 1942. Tilse and his partner, Oliver "Ollie" Bowman, operated Bend Airport from 1945 to 1951. A fire destroyed the company's hangar in late May 1946. The company lost four airplanes, which were used for flight training under the GI Bill. Construction of two new hangars was approved in 1946. (DHM.)

With the construction project on track, Bowman visited Lock Haven, Pennsylvania, to fly home a new Piper Cub trainer from the Piper Aircraft Company. Delayed several times by storms, he returned on June 10, 1946. According to an article in *The Bend Bulletin*, Bowman's actual flying time was 40 hours and 40 minutes. Pictured is Bowman with a North American Texan. (Kay Kirkbride.)

Nationally known precision flyer "Swede" Ralston was a guest at the Bend Airport for Fourth of July celebrations in the late 1940s. One of his more popular shows was called How Not to Fly, a comedy act performed in a Piper Cub. The acrobatics part of Ralston's program was done flying his North American AT-6 Texan. According to Bowman's daughter Kay, Ralston and Bowman became good friends. (*The Bend Bulletin*.)

Bend had famous visitors in 1948 when it hosted George Truman (left) and Clifford Evans (right). The pair circled the globe in their Piper Super Cruisers *City of the Angels* (pictured), and *City of Washington*. The four-month world trip covered 22,436 miles. Flags of the countries visited were hand-painted on the left side of the fuselage, and 53 of the 55 city stops are on the right side. (DHM.)

Central Oregon ranchers and farmers were constantly trying to keep coyotes away from their livestock. Government-approved hunters did their best to thin the pack of coyotes roaming the area. With the arrival of the airplane, hunters could patrol larger areas in shorter times for better control of the packs. (DHM.)

In the late 1940s, the Oregon State Game Commission allowed aerial coyote hunting in areas where ranchers were losing livestock. Tilse and Bowman, as well as other local aviators, were licensed for aerial hunting. During the early 1950s, Bowman was invited to speak on the KOIN-CBS show *Northwest Neighbors*—the topic was "I Shoot Coyotes from the Sky." Interviewed by Bob Crosby (left), Bowman told the audience, "It takes careful planning and tricky maneuvering. We pick a certain area, usually a valley, and we work back and forth until we find our quarry. We fly around 150 to 200 feet off the ground, and with enough experience you can see coyotes from that altitude. Then we get right down within 15 or 20 feet to the ground. You got to be on your toes. Lots of times we've been all set to open up only find a haystack or telephone line straight ahead, flying at about 75 miles an hour." (CBS-KOIN.)

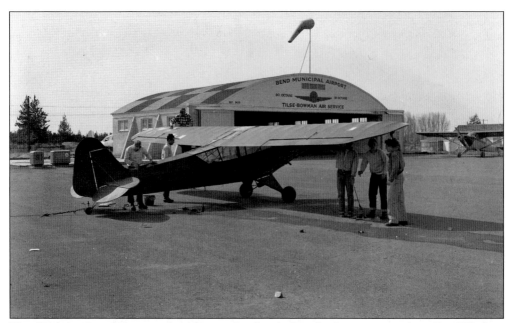

The Civil Air Patrol traces its founding to the days before the Japanese attack on Pearl Harbor. The director of the Office of Civilian Defense, Fiorello La Guardia, brought the organization into existence on December 1, 1941. CAP banded together civilian pilots under one umbrella with the mission to "provide private citizens with adequate facilities to assist in meeting local and national emergencies." During the war, CAP pilots patrolled more than 24 million miles over the Atlantic and the Gulf of Mexico to help stop the German U-boat menace. They also provided aerial courier service, spotted forest fires, and located lost planes. The CAP continued after the war and is still active. Local CAP squadrons were stationed in Redmond, Prineville, and Madras. In 1956, the Bend CAP squadron was led by airport manager Pat Gibson. Pictured here are Bend CAP volunteers outside the Tilse-Bowman hangar. (Both, DHM.)

In the March 1957 photograph above, Jerry Sheffield (left) and Pat Gibson are using the large Bend hangar to rebuild airplanes. Aimed at the mid-priced market, Central Oregon Aircraft was founded by businessman Oscar Murray, with Pat Gibson as president and *The Bend Bulletin* owner and publisher Robert Chandler as secretary. "The output will be sold on terms at moderate prices within the reach of anyone who can afford an automobile," said Gibson in an article in the March 2, 1957, issue of the Bend newspaper. The below aerial photograph captures Bend Airport in 1960 and shows the main runway and the taxi strip as well as two additional dirt landing strips. The pond was eventually filled in and the two runways disappeared. (Both, DHM.)

Bend Airport was not only a place for grown-ups, but also for kids, as noted in an article in the May 21, 1958, edition of *The Bend Bulletin*. The second annual event for schoolchildren from Young School in Bend featured an aerial sightseeing tour thanks to Gibson Air Services and pilot Jerry Sheffield. Described as an "Upsy Daisy" by the reporter, about 50 students got a taste of flying during the quick up and down trip. At left, Bobby Kohfield is ready to board the Piper Cub. Below, from left to right, Frances McWilliams, Linda Kohfield, and Karen Dyer, anxiously await their turns. (Both, DHM.)

Bend's city council has invested heavily in the municipal airport throughout the late 2010s. Although the airport is on county land, the city owns and operates the airfield. The airport sits on 420 acres and is home to over 240 aircraft. "We're busier than Redmond as far as takeoffs and landings," said Bend Municipal Airport manager Gary Judd in a 2019 interview. The airport generates roughly $174 million in roll-over dollars for the community. Demand for airport services is driven by companies doing business in Bend. Judd admitted not suffering from Redmond envy. "The overall push is for Redmond to be the commercial service airport. We don't want to compete with or pull away any of that synergy from Redmond. It is not good for the community." (Both, City of Bend.)

Barnstormers and birdmen have not lost their draw for aviation enthusiasts. People still crane their necks when they hear an airplane overhead. When the Wright brothers moved their training grounds from the sand dunes at Kitty Hawk in 1904 to Huffman Prairie in Dayton, Ohio, locals flocked to the cow pasture to watch them fly. Central Oregon is no different. The undated photograph above was likely taken at the old Bend rodeo grounds near Shevlin Park. As soon as the airplane landed, spectators crowded around it and its pilot. The photograph below captures the same excitement, with aviation enthusiasts getting a chance to look inside the front office of a US Air Force F-16 Fighting Falcon at the 1992 Redmond Air Show. (Both, DHM.)

What started as a fly-in at Ray Ochs's farm in the late 1970s became the genesis of the Air Show of the Cascades. Ochs invited pilots to land on his field as soon as the crops had been taken in. The event was moved to Madras Airport in 2000. The 20th anniversary event in 2020 was rescheduled for fall 2021 due to the COVID-19 pandemic. (Air Show of the Cascades.)

Central Oregon weather offers clear skies—the lifeblood for aviators of all eras. Madras Airport has, over the years, become a mecca for fly-ins. Over 200 spectators attended the second annual Beaver State Regional Aerobatic Precision Competition in September 1981 and got to see daring young men in their flying machines do barrel rolls, Cuban eights, and inside loops. (DHM.)

Redmond Airport became host to the short-lived biannual Central Oregon Air Show in 1988. The first two events, in 1988 and 1990, attracted 50,000 and 30,000, respectively. The main draw was the US Air Force Thunderbirds flight demonstration team. The third event in 1992 saw only 15,000 attend due to inclement weather. Although the organizers lost money that year, they came back for another show in 1994. (Author's collection.)

Sunriver Airport used to hold popular fly-ins disguised as pancake breakfasts. The 19th annual Wings and Wheels charity fly-in event in July 2013 was the last such event. At the time, the organizers expected over 2,000 people to show up, with pilots coming in from Oregon, California, Washington, Nevada, Hawaii, and Canada. (*Sunriver Scene.*)

Nine

THE BUSINESS OF FLYING

The business of flying in Central Oregon includes both the US Forest Service and private companies.

The Forest Service was an early adopter of the airplane in its fight against forest fires. In January 1921, US Army Air Corp major H.H. "Hap" Arnold, who served with distinction in both world wars, released a report called "Aerial Forest Fire Patrol—1920." Reviewing the forest fire aerial patrols over California, Oregon, and Washington, Arnold explained the use of airplanes in fire spotting: "The airplane patrol left the base about 9:00 a.m., arriving at the sub-base about 11:00 a.m. It then remained over [the forest] until about 1:00 p.m. arriving at its home station again about 3:00 p.m., so that for about four hours of twenty-four the airplane was in the air, covering some part of the national forest."

Arnold noted this might not be the best use of airplanes for fire patrol work. "It is believed that during the next season a plan of patrol will be developed which will combine the method of patrolling used with a scheme whereby the patrols will be used on special reconnaissance missions for observing and directing the fighting of large fires."

Early spotter planes, such as the single-engine DeHavilland DH4-B biplane, were considered adequate, but some pilots preferred two-engine planes to increase range in an emergency. The weakest link in the fire-spotting chain was radio equipment aboard the airplane. "Without the radio, the airplane is practically useless," Arnold wrote.

Early aviators used homing pigeons to relay messages, or simply set down close to a farmer's house to telephone the home base. A century later, Major Arnold and other early aviators involved in firefighting duties would marvel at the changes today.

From the early days of aviation, fixed-base operators have existed in a symbiotic relationship with airport management. Aviation-related businesses have provided services to pilots and their aircraft. Charter service, flight instruction, aircraft rental, refueling, and other similar businesses have become important auxiliary services. Today, airports are also a natural choice for airplane manufacturers such as Lancair International and Epic Air, based at Redmond and Bend Airports, respectively.

156139

Aerial forest fire spotting was a dangerous undertaking. Airborne for four-hour shifts, the pilots flew over their assigned areas at between 8,000–11,000 feet looking for evidence of a developing forest fire. The terrain was unforgiving, with few places to land in an emergency. Here is a DeHavilland DH-4B on patrol with Mt. Jefferson in the background in 1920. (US Army Air Service.)

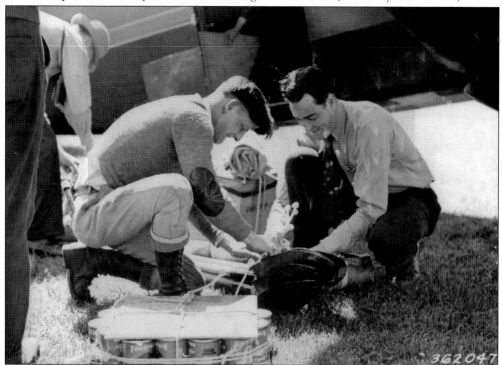

362047

Originally operating out of airfields in Eugene, Medford, and Portland in the early 1930s, the Forest Service began stationing fire-spotting planes at Bend and Redmond Airports. A June 1931 article in *The Bend Bulletin* described how airplanes also could be used to haul trucks, piece by piece, into the forest for the movement of men and equipment. These forest rangers are packing much lighter loads for supply drops to firefighters in 1937. (Deschutes National Forest.)

One of the challenges once firefighters were on the ground was to resupply missions with food and other necessities. Most supplies were delivered by trucks, but at times, airplanes were needed to make deliveries into hard-to-reach places. Precision dropping of supplies into wooded areas with parachutes was not always possible, as World War II–veteran transport pilots would quickly find out while re-supplying troops. This image was captured in 1937. (US Forest Service.)

Alden Williams was one of several flight instructors in the Bend and Redmond area. Together with Frank Stratton, he flew supply operations for the Deschutes National Forest during the summer of 1938. Operating out of a meadow at Davis Lake, Williams dropped supplies to firefighters below from his Taylor Cub. On one occasion, his plane was loaded with 200 pounds of supplies. (DHM.)

Work on a proposed central aerial firefighting operations center for the Deschutes National Forest began in earnest in 1961. Redmond was one of many candidates for the center. In the end, the size and quality of Roberts Field, in addition to favorable weather conditions, made Redmond the ideal location. Redmond Air Center was dedicated in August 1964. Throughout the 1960s, additional buildings were added, among them administrative offices, barracks, training facilities including a paraloft for smoke jumpers, a warehouse for a regional fire cache, and two hangars. By 1970, the center was built out according to the original plans. Over the years, additional construction has added modernized administration and training buildings. (Both, Deschutes National Forest.)

This Short 330 Sherpa was introduced in the 1990s and followed a long line of venerable airplanes used for smoke jumping operations. The Forest Service utilized Ford Trimotors from 1942 to 1969 and DC-3 Dakotas from the mid-1940s through the early 2000s. The Short Sherpa was originally designed as a regional airliner with space for 30 passengers. (DHM.)

Plans to use dirigibles to transport firefighters into remote areas were considered in the early 1920s. Quickly abandoned, it would be almost two decades before smoke jumping was tried again. In June 1940, assistant regional forester Melvin Merritt with the US Forest Service Pacific Northwest Region office in Portland reported trials of "unloading firefighters from airplanes" in Chelan National Forest. (Deschutes National Forest.)

Smoke jumpers go through rigorous training in preparation for dropping in on an active forest fire. Every year, before the fire season starts, smoke jumpers must be recertified, which includes two jumps. On an active jump, the firefighter carries 130 pounds of equipment and supplies. Once their assignment ends, everything has to be carried out. At right, a visiting student tries on a pack-out bag. (DHM.)

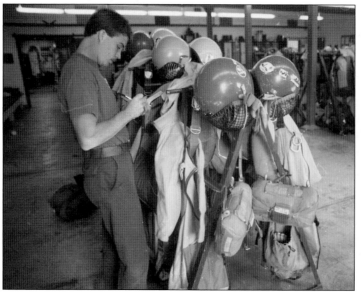

The Redmond Air Center has a cavernous equipment center where firefighters patch up their jumpsuits and parachutes. Here, Daren Hallady is inventorying the many parachutes stored in the ready room. The summer of 1993 was reportedly one of the slowest fire seasons in the Oregon and Washington area in many years. Normally, smoke jumpers averaged 300 hours of overtime. In 1993, that amount was halved. (DHM.)

On the other side of battling fires from the air are the fire bombers. In early tests in the 1920s, fire retardants in bottles were dropped over test fires. Cal Butler operated an aerial firefighting service at Redmond Airport from 1957 to the time of his death in 2004. Above is a DC-7B from Butler Aircraft in the early 1990s with, from left to right, Charles "Chuck" Sheridan, Tom Raider, Skip Alderson, Bob Webb, and Brian Lash. (DHM.)

Airborne firefighting is risky business. This DC-7B (N848D) was involved in a tragic accident on October 1, 1992, when the plane crashed during firefighting operations in Eldorado National Forest. Both the pilot, Chuck Sheridan of Porterville, California, and first officer Leonard Martin of Exeter, California, perished. They were employed by TBM Inc. of Tulare, California, flying under a Forest Service contract. (DHM.)

Private companies also contract with government entities to fight fires. During the busy fire season of 1994, the US Bureau of Land Management (BLM) was scrambling to locate equipment to fight wildfires in Ochoco National Forest. Help came in the form of a Polish Mielec Melex, or the Dromedary M-18. Operated by Western Pilot Services of Phoenix, Arizona, the single-seat aircraft was capable of dousing fires with its 450-gallon load of fire retardants. (DHM.)

Central Oregonians are dependent on the major highways in and out of the area for travel and freight. Accidents are bound to happen on the roads crossing the Cascade Mountains. Every minute is critical for victims of auto accidents. Quickly accessing hard-to-reach accident sites, AirLink, owned by Denton, Texas–based, for-profit Med-Trans Corporation, operates an air ambulance service from St. Charles Medical Center's helipad in Bend. (DHM.)

Central Oregon's airports brim with aviation companies taking advantage of the area's excellent flying conditions. In 1991, Lance Niebauer, the owner of Lancair, moved its operations from Santa Paula, California, to Redmond, where the company produces kit planes for pilots with a flair for homebuilding. The company sold 200 kit planes that year. (Lancair.)

Carsten Sundin of Bend is one of Lancair's many clients. According to a 1991 interview, he estimated it would take 1,500 man hours to build his Lancair ES. In 1997, Lancair built a $5 million plant in Bend to build turn-key aircraft, the Columbia 300. During the Great Recession of 2007–2009, Lancair closed its Bend operations. The company finally settled in Uvalde, Texas, although the Endeavour line is still produced in Redmond. (Author's collection.)

The rich history of local fixed-based operators at Central Oregon airports has continued with Leading Edge Aviation, a flight service company operating out of Bend Municipal Airport. The company's light-green helicopters have become a familiar sight in the skies over Central Oregon as student pilots learn the ins and outs of rotorcraft operations. Together with Central Oregon Community College, Leading Edge has classrooms and operates a flight simulator at the college (below). The company offers a two-year associate degree program in aviation science. Jack Warner, vice president of the flight academy, praises the Central Oregon weather, which allows students to experience everything from sunny-day flying to thunderstorms and icy winter days. (Both, Leading Edge Aviation.)

Ten

REDMOND
REGIONAL AIRPORT

More than a century after the Wright Flyer left terra firma under its own power, the business of aviation has radically changed. From the time of flimsy propeller-driven barnstormer planes to passenger jets, generations of Central Oregonians have relied on the airplane to see their hometown from above or fly to domestic or international destinations.

At the time of the production of this book, the future of air travel is not clear. In January 2020, officials at the Redmond Municipal Airport were looking forward to a year with over a million passengers moving through the airport. The COVID-19 pandemic, which struck soon after, reduced that forecast to a trickle.

World wars, economic depressions and recessions, oil embargoes, terror attacks, and other unforeseeable circumstances have affected air travel before. Despite such calamities, people have always returned to flying.

According to the Los Angeles–based Milken Institute, the Bend-Redmond metropolitan area snagged the top position as the "Best Performing Small City in the Country" for the fourth year in a row in 2020.

Diversifying the local economy, coupled with a focus on the regional airport in Redmond, has helped turn rural Central Oregon into an economic powerhouse. Economic Development for Central Oregon, a regional nonprofit corporation backed by private and public stakeholders, is helping to attract industry clusters such as high-tech, outdoor, food, and to some extent, bioscience, to the area. Economic diversification is in addition to strengthening existing industries.

Tourism is also benefitting from fast connections in and out of the area. Central Oregon has been a tourist mecca since the early part of the 20th century. Tourist dollars have supported the area during both good and bad times.

There are many reasons to believe Redmond Municipal Airport, better known locally as Roberts Field, or by the airport code RDM, will continue to serve the Central Oregon community in the coming decades.

The old Redmond terminal building was replaced in December 1980. However, it was almost a full year before the formal dedication took place. The event was marred by bad weather. The newspaper reporter wrote, "You couldn't have asked for a worse day to dedicate an airport terminal." The planned air show scheduled by the Oregon Air National Guard had to be canceled, and the Kiwanis barbecue proved a wet event. The dedication of the new building included the unveiling of Sisters sculptor J.C. "Skip" Armstrong's bronze sculpture *Cycles of Life* (below). Mayor Sam Johnson gave "strict orders" not to unveil the sculpture until the dedication of the airport. (Both, DHM.)

On October 11, 1981, the community gathered to hear Redmond mayor Sam Johnson reminisce about J.R. Roberts and his determination to set Central Oregon on the path to a regional airport. "[Roberts] could be seen picking rocks off the crude airstrip in the earliest days of the facility." At the dedication, Mayor Johnson recalled the first time he soloed at Redmond in the 1930s: "[The] field was just a strip," he noted. "But Roberts helped get WPA grants which were needed to get the plan moving." At the time of the inauguration of the new terminal building in 1981, Central Oregon was serviced by Republic Airlines and Air Oregon (below). (Both, DHM.)

It did not take long before the new passenger terminal became too small for the increasing flow of traffic. Between 1986 and 1987, the number of passengers utilizing the terminal building doubled. Passengers boarding and deplaning hit approximately 140,000. In 1987, Redmond Airport manager Jerry Zimmer (below, left) and Mayor Bob Riggs (right) began to secure funding for an enlarged airport terminal, increased parking, and a dedicated fire hall. The infrastructure improvements were aimed to set up the airport for future expansion, something that would benefit area companies. The FAA agreed to pay half of the $2.4 million of the project costs, but Redmond was responsible for the rest. Local officials hoped to apply for $600,000 of regional lottery money and reach out to local businesses for the other $600,000. (Both, DHM.)

City officials were betting the expanded terminal would attract a third airline to Redmond Airport. As of August 1989, Horizon Air and United Express were flying to and from Roberts Field. With the new terminal almost ready in 1993, the Central Oregon Task Force was lobbying Reno Air and Morris Air to establish roots at Roberts Field. Reno Air signed on in May 1995 and offered jet service to Los Angeles. It was the early 2000s before Redmond Airport started seeing additional airlines establishing stable roots. Above is a United Express British Aerospace twin-turboprop Jetstream 3101. In the background, the new terminal building is under construction. Below is a Horizon Airlines twin-turboprop Fairchild Swearingen Metroliner. (Both, DHM.)

Carrie Novick (above) served as Redmond's airport manager from 1990 to 2011 and oversaw several modernization projects at the airport. The official groundbreaking for the expanded and updated terminal building took place in July 1992. As construction of the $3.9 million project was running full steam, Novick also dealt with an overhaul of runway 4-22. The 15-year-old surface "is coming apart, not just on the surface, but underneath," said Novick in a December 1992 article in *The Bulletin*. The project also saw the installation of energy-efficient runway lights and an emergency generator to provide backup power for the airport's instrument landing system. When the project got underway the following summer, scheduled flights were diverted to Bend Municipal Airport (below). Passengers had to drive to Redmond to check in for their flight, then take a bus to Bend for departure. (Both, DHM.)

This picture captures the frustrating, year-long construction project at Roberts Field. Departing and arriving passengers had to work around temporary gates and other obstructions to fly in and out of Central Oregon. The terminal construction was not without drama. Central Oregon was hit with the worst snowstorm in a century, which delayed construction for three months and also warranted a redesign of the sloping roofs to withstand snow loads. (DHM.)

THE MOST ASKED QUESTIONS
ABOUT THE TERMINAL PROJECT:
PARKING LOT/ROAD COMPLETION DATE: JUNE 1993
1ST PHASE TERMINAL OCT. 1ST 1993
2ND PHASE TERMINAL NOV. 1ST 1993
COMPLETION JAN. 15, 1994.
THANK YOU FOR YOUR PATIENCE AND COOPERATION
DURING OUR EXPANSION PROJECT

The terminal building was expanded from 7,971 to 23,000 square feet. The new building was formally opened to the public in November 1993 and featured high, vaulted ceilings with skylights, a massive lava rock wall, a large passenger waiting area on the second floor, and a new luggage carousel with plenty of space for arriving passengers. (DHM.)

Redmond Municipal Airport has seen further expansions since 1993, with added routes to Seattle, Los Angeles, Salt Lake City, Phoenix, and Denver. Further terminal expansion projects, as well as ramp and runway upgrades, have kept up with increasing passenger demand. (Author's collection.)

Construction of the tower, seen in the background, was not without controversy; private pilots grumbled at the potential loss of the existing flight service station, which monitored flight plans and handled in-flight communications and weather briefings. Fred Isaacs, FAA's Northwest Region administrator, assured private pilots the FAA's weather service would be just as good. (Author's collection.)

What the future holds for Redmond Airport is uncertain. From 2015 to 2020, traffic doubled from 500,000 to one million passengers. The forecast for 2021 was about one million arriving and departing passengers, but the airport ran at 50 percent compared to 2020 as a result of the COVID-19 pandemic. It may take years to recover the loss in passenger traffic. (Author's collection.)

Officials at Roberts Field began planning for the future of the airport in 2017, as part of the airport's master plan required by the FAA. Top priorities include a larger waiting area for departing passengers, covered jet bridges with direct access to aircraft, and space for larger airplanes. As of 2021, airport manager Zachary Bass hoped to start construction within the next two years. (Author's collection.)

A red line goes through the development of aviation in Central Oregon, and it is John Roy Roberts, known as "J.R." Born in Iowa in 1882, his journey west was prompted by his good friend pharmacist Maurice Lynch moving to Portland. The two moved to Redmond in 1910 and began the partnership Lynch & Roberts, a general dry goods store. Roberts became the driving force behind the Redmond Chamber of Commerce's push to develop an airport. During the 1930s, with the Great Depression putting a damper on infrastructure projects, Roberts cajoled local and state officials as well as private businesspeople to help make the airport a reality. Roberts's overarching goal was presented in a March 1938 article in *The Redmond Spokesman*: "While at the present time an airport is of little consequence in this section, we believe the work already done will be of great value in the near future. It is believed that before many years there will be air service east of the Cascades and the Redmond Airport will play an important part in the operation of such service." (J.R. Roberts.)

Described as a quiet man by his granddaughter Margaret Schinkel, *The Bend Bulletin* provided the most precise description of Roberts, also known as "Mister Aviation": "Merchant, former mayor, member of the Oregon Board of Aeronautics, a non-flyer." With his interest in aviation, it is remarkable that he never learned to fly. Here, he is "learning to fly a C-46," according to a note in his personal photo album. (J.R. Roberts.)

Mister Aviation was honored by the Oregon State Board of Aeronautics in February 1967 with the first award for distinguished service to aviation. The day after his passing on June 15, 1970, *The Bulletin* noted, "JR was a man of considerable vision. It took vision in 1910 to have faith in the future of a small Western town in an out-of-the-way area. He saw an airplane and believed it had a future." (J.R. Roberts.)

BIBLIOGRAPHY

The Bend Bulletin and *The Bulletin*, collected articles, 1907–2021.

Bednarek, Janet R. Daly. *America's Airports: Airfield Development, 1918–1947*. College Station, TX: Texas A&M University Press, 2001.

Corn, Joseph J. *The Winged Gospel: America's Romance with Aviation, 1900–1950*. Baltimore, MD: Johns Hopkins University Press, 2002.

Goldstone, Lawrence. *Birdmen: The Wright Brothers, Glenn Curtiss, and the Battle to Control the Skies*. New York, NY: Ballantine, 2015.

Hanson, Tor. *Camp Abbot*. Charleston, SC: Arcadia Publishing, 2018.

———. *Sunriver*. Charleston, SC: Arcadia Publishing, 2018.

Joslin, Les. *Deschutes National Forest*. Charleston, SC: Arcadia Publishing, 2017.

McCullough, David. *The Wright Brothers*. New York, NY: Simon & Schuster, 2015.

The Redmond Spokesman, collected articles, 1920–1947.

Rose, Alexander. *Empires of the Sky: Zeppelins, Airplanes, and Two Men's Epic Duel to Rule the World*. New York, NY: Random House, 2021.

INDEX

DISCOVER THOUSANDS OF LOCAL HISTORY BOOKS
FEATURING MILLIONS OF VINTAGE IMAGES

Arcadia Publishing, the leading local history publisher in the United States, is committed to making history accessible and meaningful through publishing books that celebrate and preserve the heritage of America's people and places.

Find more books like this at
www.arcadiapublishing.com

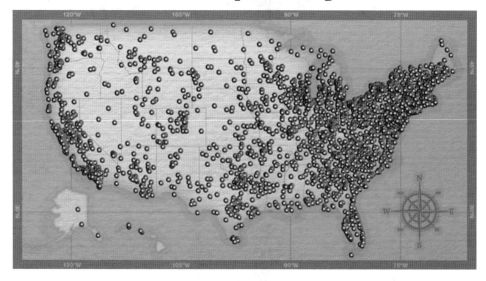

Search for your hometown history, your old stomping grounds, and even your favorite sports team.